ISBN 978-1-333-03729-1
PIBN 10456600

1 MONTH OF
FREE
READING

at
www.ForgottenBooks.com

By purchasing this book you are eligible for one month membership to ForgottenBooks.com, giving you unlimited access to our entire collection of over 1,000,000 titles via our web site and mobile apps.

To claim your free month visit:
www.forgottenbooks.com/free456600

THE
AUTHOR's FARCE;
WITH A
PUPPET-SHOW;
CALL'D THE
PLEASURES *of the* TOWN.

As Acted at the

THEATRE ROYAL in *Drury-Lane.*

Written by *HENRY FIELDING*, Efq;

—————— Quis iniquæ
Tam patiens urbis, tam ferreus, ut teneat fe ?
/ Juv. Sat. 1.

The THIRD EDITION.

This PIECE was Originally Acted at the *Hay-Market*, and
Revived fome Years after at *Drury-Lane*, when it was Revifed,
and greatly Alter'd by the AUTHOR, as now Printed.

LONDON:

Printed for J. WATTS at the Printing-Office in
Wild-Court near *Lincoln's-Inn Fields.*

MDCCL. Price 1s. 6d.

PROLOGUE.

Spoken by Mr. *JONES*.

TOO *long the Tragick Muse hath aw'd the Stage,*
And frightned Wives and Children with her Rage.
Too long Drawcanſir *roars,* Parthenope *weeps,*
While ev'ry Lady cries, and Critick ſleeps.
With Ghoſts, Rapes, Murders, tender Hearts they wound,
Or elſe, like Thunder, terrify with Sound.
When the skill'd Actreſs to her weeping Eyes,
With artful Sigh, the Handkerchief applies,
How griev'd each Sympathizing Nymph appears?
And Box and Gallery both melt in Tears.
Or, when in Armour of Corinthian *Braſs,*
Heroick Actor ſtares you in the Face,
And cries aloud with Emphaſis that's fit, on
Liberty, Freedom, Liberty and Briton *;*
While frowning, gaping for Applauſe he ſtands,
What generous Briton *can refuſe his Hands?*
Like the tame Animals deſign'd for Show,
You have your Cues to clap, as they to bow?
Taught to commend, your Judgments have no Share ;
By Chance you gueſs aright, by Chance you err.

But Handkerchiefs and Britain *laid aſide,*
T' Night we mean to laugh, and not to chide.

PROLOGUE.

In Days of Yore, when Fools were held in Fashion,
Tho' now, alas! all banish'd from the Nation,
A merry Jester had reform'd his Lord,
Who wou'd have scorn'd the sterner Stoick's Word.

Bred in Democritus *his laughing Schools,*
Our Author flies sad Heraclitus' *Rules:*
No Tears, no Terror plead in his Behalf;
The aim of Farce is but to make you laugh.
Beneath the Tragick or the Comick Name,
Farces and Puppet-shows ne'er miss of Fame.
Since then, in borrow'd Dress, they've pleased the Town;
Condemn them not, appearing in their own.

Smiles we expect, from the Good-natur'd few;
As ye are done by, ye Malicious, do;
And kindly laugh at him, who laughs at you.

Perſons

Persons in the FARCE.

MEN.

Luckless, *the Author and Master of the Show,*   } Mr. *Mullart.*

Witmore, *his Friend,*   Mr. *Lacy.*

Marplay *sen.*   } *Comedians.*   { Mr. *Reynolds,*

Marplay *jun.*   Mr. *Stopler.*

Bookweight, a *Bookseller,*   Mr. *Jones.*

Scarecrow,   Mr. *Marshal.*

Dash,   Mr. *Hallam.*

Quibble,   } *Scriblers.*   Mr. *Dove.*

Blotpage,   Mr. *Wells,* Jun.

Index,

Jack, *Servant to* Luckless,   Mr. *Achurch.*

Jack-Pudding,   Mr. *Reynolds.*

Bantomite,   Mr. *Marshal.*

WOMEN.

Mrs. Moneywood, *the Author's Landlady,*   } Mrs. *Mullart.*

Harriot, *her Daughter,*   Miss *Palms.*

Person

Persons in the PUPPET-SHOW.

Player,	Mr. *Dove.*
Conftable,	Mr. *Wells.*
Murder-text, *A Presbyterian Parfon,*	Mr. *Hallam.*
Goddefs of Nonfenfe,	Mrs. *Mullart.*
Charon,	Mr. *Ayres.*
Curry, *a Bookfeller,*	Mr. *Dove.*
A Poet,	Mr. *W. Hallam.*
Signior Opera,	Mr. *Stopler.*
Don Tragedio,	Mr. *Marfhal,*
Sir Farcical Comick,	Mr. *Davenport.*
Dr. Orator,	Mr. *Jones.*
Monfieur Pantomime,	Mr. *Knott.*
Mrs. Novel,	Mrs. *Martin.*
Robgrave, *the Sexton,*	Mr. *Harris.*
Sailor,	Mr. *Achurch.*
Somebody,	Mr. *Harris,* Jun.
Nobody,	Mr. *Wells,* Jun.
Punch,	Mr. *Reynolds.*
Joan,	Mr. *Hicks.*
Lady Kingcall,	Mifs *Clarke.*
Mrs. Cheat'em,	Mrs. *Wind.*
Mrs. Glafs-ring,	Mrs. *Blunt.*
Count Ugly,	

THE

THE
AUTHOR's FARCE.

ACT I. SCENE I.

Luckless's Room in Mrs. Moneywood's *House.*

Mrs. Moneywood, Harriot, Luckless.

MONEYWOOD.

EVER tell me, Mr. *Luckless*, of your Play, and your Play. I tell you, I muſt be paid. I would no more depend on a Benefit-Night of an unacted Play, than I would on a Benefit-Ticket in an undrawn Lottery. Cou'd I have gueſs'd that I had a Poet in my Houſe! Cou'd I have look'd for a Poet under lac'd Clothes!

Luck. Why not? ſince you may often find Poverty under them: Nay, they are commonly the Signs of it: And therefore, why may not a Poet be ſeen in them as well as a Courtier?

Money. Do you make a Jeſt of my Misfortune, Sir?

Luck. Rather *my* Misfortune. I am ſure I have a better Title to Poverty than you; for notwithſtanding the handſom Figure I make, unleſs you are ſo good to invite me, I am afraid I ſhall ſcarce prevail on my Stomach to dine to-day.

Money.

Money. O never fear that; you will never want a Dinner till you have dined at all the Eating-houfes round. —— No one fhuts their Doors againft you the firft time; and I think you are fo kind, feldom to trouble them a fecond.

Luck. No—— And if you will give me leave to walk out of *your* Doors, the Devil take me if ever I come into 'em again.

Money. Pay me, Sir, what you owe me, and walk away whenever you pleafe.

Luck. With all my Heart, Madam; get me a Pen and Ink, and I'll give you my Note for it immediately.

Money. Your Note! Who will difcount it? Not your Bookfeller, for he has as many of your Notes as he has of your Works, Both good lafting Ware, and which are never likely to go out of his Shop, and his Scrutore.

Har. Nay, but Madam, 'tis barbarous to infult him in this manner.

Money. No doubt you'll take his Part. Pray, get you about your Bufinefs. I fuppofe he intends to pay me, by ruining you. Get you in, this Inftant, and remember if ever I fee you with him again, I'll turn you out of Doors.

S   C   E   N   E   II.

Lucklefs, *Mrs.* Moneywood.

Luck. Difcharge all your Ill-nature on me, Madam, but fpare poor Mifs *Harriot.*

Money. Oh! then it is plain. I have fufpected your Familiarity a long while. You are a bafe Man. Is it not enough to ftay three Months in my Houfe without paying me a Farthing, but you muft ruin my Child?

Luck. I love her as my Soul. Had I the World, I'd give it her all.

Money. But as you happen to have nothing in the World, I defire you would have nothing to fay to her. I fuppofe you wou'd have fettled all your Caftles in the Air. Oh! I wifh you had liv'd in one of them, inftead

of

of my Houfe. Well, I am refolv'd, when you are gone away (which I heartily hope will be very foon) I'll hang over my Door in great red Letters, *No Lodgings for Poets.*
—— Sure, never was fuch a Gueft as you have been. My Floor is all fpoil'd with Ink, my Windows with Verfes, and my Door has been almoft beat down with Duns.

Luck. Would your Houfe had been beaten down, and every thing, but my dear *Harriot,* crufh'd under it.

Money. Sir, Sir——

Luck. Madam, Madam! I will attack you at your own Weapons; I will pay you in your own Coin.

Money. I wifh you wou'd pay me in any Coin, Sir.

Luck. Look ye, Madam, I'll do as much as a reafonable Woman can require; I'll fhew you all I have; and give you all I have too, if you pleafe to accept it.
[*Turns his Pockets infide out.*

Money. I will not be us'd in this manner. No, Sir, I will be paid, if there be any fuch thing as Law.

Luck. By what Law you will put Money into my Pocket, I know not; for I never heard of any one who got Money by the Law, but the Lawyers. I have told you already, and, I tell you again, that the firft Money I get fhall be yours; and I have great Expectations from my Play. In the mean time, your ftaying here can be of no Service, and you may poffibly drive fome fine Thoughts out of my Head. I wou'd write a Love-Scene, and your Daughter wou'd be more proper Company on that Occafion, than you.

Money. You wou'd act a Love-Scene, I believe, but I fhall prevent you; for I intend to difpofe of myfelf, before my Daughter.

Luck. Difpofe of yourfelf!

Money. Yes, Sir, difpofe of myfelf—— 'Tis very well known, that I have had very good Offers fince my laft dear Husband died. I might have had an Attorney of *New-Inn,* or Mr. *Fiill-pot* the Excife-man: Yes, I had my Choice of two Parfons, or a Doctor of Phyfick; and yet I flighted them all; yes I flighted them for—— for——for you.   *Luck.*

Luck. For me!

Money. Yes, you have feen too vifible Marks of my Paffion; too vifible for my Reputation.   [*Sobbing.*

Luck. I have heard very loud Tokens of your Paffion; but I rather took it for the Paffion of Anger, than of Love.

Money. Oh! it was Love indeed: Nothing but Love upon my Soul.

Luck. The Devil! This way of Dunning is worfe than the other.

Money. If thou canft not pay me in Money, let me have it in Love.—If I break through the Modefty of my Sex, let my Paffion excufe it—— I know the World will call it an impudent Action; but if you will let me referve all I have to myfelf, I will make myfelf yours for ever.

Luck. Toll, loll, loll!

Money. And is this the manner you receive my Declaration, you poor beggarly Fellow? You fhall repent this, remember you fhall repent it, remember that. I'll fhew you the Revenge of an injur'd Woman.

Luck. I fhall never repent any thing that rids me of you, I am fure.

SCENE III.

Luckless, Harriot.

Luck. Dear *Harriot!*

Har. I have waited an Opportunity to return to you.

Luck. Oh! my Dear, I am fo fick.

Har. What's the matter?

Luck. Oh! your Mother! your Mother!

Har. What, has fhe been Scolding ever fince?

Luck. Worfe! worfe!

Har. Heav'n forbid, fhe fhould threaten to go to Law with you.

Luck. Oh, worfe! worfe! She threatens to go to Church with me. She has made me a generous Offer, that if I will but marry her, fhe will fuffer me to fettle all fhe has upon her.   *Har.*

Har. Generous Creature! Sure you will not refift the Propofal?

Luck. Hum! what wou'd you advife me to?

Har. Oh, take her, take her, by all means; you will be the prettieft, fineft, lovelieft, fweeteft Couple— Auh! what a delicate Difh of Matrimony you will make? Her Age with your Youth, her Avarice with your Extravagance, and her Scolding with your Poetry.

Luck. Nay, but I am ferious, and I defire you wou'd be fo. You know my unhappy Circumftances, and your Mother's Wealth. It would be at leaft a prudent Match.

Har. Oh! extremely prudent, ha, ha, ha, the World will fay, Lard! who could have thought Mr. *Luckless* had had fo much Prudence. This one Action will over-balance all the Follies of your Life.

Luck. Faith, I think it will: But, dear *Harriot*, how can I think of lofing you for ever? And yet as our Affairs ftand, I fee no Poffibility of our being happy together. It will be fome Pleafure too, that I may have it in my Power to ferve you. Believe me it is with the utmoft Reluctance I think of parting with you: For if it was in my Power to have you——

Har. Oh, I am very much oblig'd to you —— I believe you—Yes, you need not fwear, I believe you.

Luck. And can you as eafily confult Prudence, and part with me? for I wou'd not buy my own Happinefs at the Price of yours.

Har. I thank you, Sir,——part with you— intolerable Vanity!

Luck. Then I am refolv'd, and fo, my good Landlady, have at you.

Har. Stay, Sir, let me acquaint you with one thing; you are a Villain! and don't think I'm vex'd at any thing, but that I fhou'd have been fuch a Fool, as ever to have had a good Opinion of you. [*Crying.*

Luck. Ha, ha, ha! Caught by *Jupiter* ! And did my dear *Harriot* think me in Earneft?

Har. And was you not in Earneft?

Luck.

Luck. What, to part with thee? A pretty Woman will be sooner in Earnest to part with her Beauty, or a great Man with his Power.

Har. I wish I were assur'd of the Sincerity of your Love.

A I R. *Butter'd Peaſe.*

Luck. *Does my deareſt* Harriot *ask*
   What for Love I wou'd purſue?
Wou'd you, Charmer, know what Task
   I wou'd undertake for you?

Ask the bold Ambitious, what
   He for Honours wou'd atchieve?
Or the gay Voluptuous, that
   Which he'd not for Pleaſure give?

Ask the Miſer what he'd do,
   To amaſs exceſſive Gain?
Or the Saint, what he'd purſue,
   His wiſh'd Heav'n to obtain?

Theſe I wou'd attempt, and more:
   For Oh! my Harriot *is to me,*
All Ambition, Pleaſure, Store,
   Or what Heav'n itſelf can be!

Har. *Wou'd my deareſt* Luckleſs *know,*
   What his conſtant Harriot *can*
Her tender Love and Faith to ſhow,
   For her dear, her only Man.

Ask the vain Coquette, what ſhe
   For Mens Adoration wou'd;
Or from Cenſure to be free,
   Ask the vile cenſorious Prude.

In a Coach and Six to ride,
   What the mercenary Jade,
Or the Widow to be Bride
   To a brisk broad-ſhoulder'd Blade.

All

All thefe I wou'd attempt for thee,
Cou:d I but thy Paffion fix;
Thy Will, my fole Commander be,
And thy Arms my Coach and Six.

Money. [*within.*] *Harriot, Harriot.*

Har. Hear the dreadful Summons, adieu. I will take the firft Opportunity of feeing you again.

Luck. Adieu, my pretty Charmer; go thy ways for the firft of thy Sex.

S C E N E IV.

Lucklefs, Jack.

Luck. So! What News bring you!

Jack. An't pleafe your Honour, I have been at my Lord's, and his Lordfhip thanks you for the Favour you have offer'd of reading your Play to him; but he has fuch a prodigious deal of Bufinefs, he begs to be excus'd. I have been with Mr. *Keyber* too: He made me no Anfwer at all. Mr. *Bookweight* will be here immediately.

Luck. *Jack.*

Jack. Sir.

Luck. Fetch my other Hat hither. Carry it to the Pawnbrokers.

Jack. To your Honour's own Pawnbroker.

Luck. Ay——And in thy way home, call at the Cook's Shop. So, one way or other I find, my Head muft always provide for my Belly.

S C E N E. V.

Lucklefs, Witmore.

Luck. I am furprifed! dear *Witmore!*

Wit. Dear *Harry!*

Luck. This is kind, indeed; but I do not more wonder at finding a Man in this Age, who can be a

Friend

Friend to Adverſity, than that Fortune ſhould be ſo much my Friend, as to direct you to me; for ſhe is a Lady I have not been much indebted to lately.

Wi. She who told me, I aſſure you, is one you have been indebted to a long while.

Luck. Whom do you mean?

Wit. One who complains of your Unkindneſs in not Viſiting her; Mrs. *Lovewood.*

Luck. Doſt thou viſit there ſtill, then?

Wit. I throw an idle Hour away there ſometimes. When I am in an ill Humour, I am ſure of feeding it there with all the Scandal in Town; for no Bawd is half ſo diligent in looking after Girls with an uncrack'd Maidenhead, as ſhe in ſearching out Women with crack'd Reputations.

Luck. The much more infamous Office, of the two.

Wit. Thou art ſtill a Favourer of the Women, I find.

Luck. Ay, the Women and the Muſes; the high Roads to Beggary.

Wit. What, art thou not cured of Scribling yet?

Luck. No, Scribling is as impoſſible to cure as the Gout.

Wit. And as ſure a Sign of Poverty as the Gout of Riches. 'Sdeath! in an Age of Learning and true Politeneſs, where a Man might ſucceed by his Merit, there would be ſome Encouragement. But now, when Party and Prejudice carry all before them, when Learning is decried, Wit not underſtood, when the Theatres are Puppet-Shows, and the Comedians Ballad-Singers: When Fools lead the Town, wou'd a Man think to thrive by his Wit? If you muſt write, write Nonſenſe, write Operas, write *Hurlo-thrumbo's,* ſet up an *Oratory* and preach Nonſenſe; and you may meet with Encouragement enough. Be profane, be ſcurrilous, be immodeſt; if you wou'd receive Applauſe, deſerve to receive Sentence at the *Old-Baily:* And if you wou'd ride in a Coach, deſerve to ride in a Cart.

Luck.

Luck. You are warm, my Friend.

Wit. It is becaufe I am your Friend. I cannot bear to hear the Man I love ridiculed by Fools, by Idiots— To hear a Fellow, who had he been born a *Chinefe,* had ftarv'd for want of Genius, to have been even the loweft Mechanick, tofs up his empty Noddle with an affected Difdain of what he has not underftood; and Women abufing what they have neither feen nor read, from an unreafonable Prejudice to an honeft Fellow, whom they have not known. If thou wilt write againft all thefe Reafons get a Patron, be Pimp to fome worthlefs Man of Quality, write Panegyricks on him, flatter him with as many Virtues as he has Vices: Then perhaps you will engage his Lordfhip, his Lordfhip engages the Town on your Side, and then write till your Arms ake, Senfe or Nonfenfe, it will all go down.

Luck. Thou art too fatirical on Mankind. It is poffible to thrive in the World by juftifiable Means.

Wit. Ay, juftifiable, and fo they are juftifiable by Cuftom. What does the Soldier or Phyfician thrive by, but Slaughter? The Lawyer, but by Quarrels? The Courtier, but by Taxes? The Poet, but by Flattery? I know none that thrive by profiting Mankind, but the Husbandman, and the Merchant: The one gives you the Fruit of your own Soil, the other brings you thofe from Abroad; and yet thefe are reprefented as mean and mechanical, and the others as honourable and glorious.

Luck. Well, but prithee leave Railing, and tell me what you wou'd advife me to do?

Wit. Do! why, thou art a vigorous young Fellow, and there are rich Widows in Town.

Luck. But I am already engaged.

Wit. Why don't you marry then——for I fuppofe you are not mad enough to have any Engagement with a poor Miftrefs.

Luck. Even fo, faith, and fo heartily that I wou'd not change her for the Widow of a *Crœfus.*

Wit.

Wit. Now thou art undone, indeed. Matrimony clenches Ruin beyond Retrieval. What unfortunate Stars wert thou born under! Was it not enough to follow thofe nine ragged Jades the Mufes, but you muft faften on fome Earth-born Miftrefs as poor as them?

Mar. jun. [*within.*] Order my Chairmen to call on me at St. *James's*—No, let 'em ftay.

Wit. Heyday! whom the Devil have we here?

Luck. The young Captain, Sir, no lefs Perfon, I affure you.

SCENE VI.

Luckless, Witmore, Marplay *junior.*

Mar. jun. Mr. *Luckless*, I kifs your Hands — Sir, I am your moft obedient humble Servant; you fee, Mr. *Luckless*, what Power you have over me. I attend your Commands, tho' feveral Perfons of Quality have ftaid at Court for me above this Hour.

Luck. I am obliged to you—I have a Tragedy for your Houfe, Mr. *Marplay.*

Mar. jun. Ha! If you will fend it to me, I will give you my Opinion of it, and if I can make any Alterations in it that will be for its Advantage, I will do it freely.

Wit. Alterations, Sir?

Mar. jun. Yes, Sir, Alterations—I will maintain it, let a Play be never fo good, without Alteration it will do nothing.

Wit. Very odd indeed.

Mar. jun. Did you ever write, Sir?

Wit. No, Sir, I thank Heav'n.

Mar. jun. Oh! your humble Servant—your very humble Servant, Sir. When you write yourfelf, you will find the Neceffity of Alterations. Why, Sir, wou'd you guefs that I had alter'd *Shakefpear?*

Wit. Yes faith, Sir, no one fooner.

Mar. jun. Alack-a-day! Was you to fee the Plays when they are brought to us, a Parcel of crude, un-

digefted

digefted Stuff. We are the Perfons, Sir, who lick them
into Form, that mould them into Shape——The Poet
make the Play indeed! The Colour-man might be as
well faid to make the Picture, or the Weaver the Coat:
My Father and I, Sir, are a Couple of poetical Tailors;
when a Play is brought us, we confider it as a Tailor does
his Coat, we cut it, Sir, we cut it: And let me tell you,
we have the exact Meafure of the Town, we know how
to fit their Tafte. The Poets between you and me, are
a Pack of ignorant——

Wit. Hold, hold, Sir. This is not quite fo civil to
Mr. *Luckless*: Befides, as I take it, you have done the
Town the Honour of writing yourfelf.

Mar. jun. Sir, you are a Man of Senfe, and exprefs
yourfelf well. I did, as you fay, once make a fmall
Sally into *Parnaffus*, took a fort of flying Leap over
Helicon: But if ever they catch me there again——
Sir, the Town have a Prejudice to my Family; for if
any Play cou'd have made them afhamed to damn it,
mine muft. It was all over Plot. It wou'd have made
half a dozen Novels: Nor was it cram'd with a pack of
Wit-traps, like *Congreve*, and *Wycherly*, where every one
knows when the Joke was coming. I defy the fharpeft
Critick of 'em all to have known when any Jokes of mine
were coming. The Dialogue was plain, eafy, and natural,
and not one fingle Joke in it from the Beginning to the
End: Befides, Sir, there was one Scene of tender me-
lancholy Converfation, enough to have melted a Heart of
Stone; and yet they damn'd it: And they damn'd them-
felves; for they fhall have no more of mine.

Wit. Take pity on the Town, Sir.

Mar. jun. I! No, Sir, no. I'll write no more. No
more; unlefs I am forc'd to it.

Luck. That's no eafy thing, *Marplay.*

Mar. jun. Yes, Sir. Odes, Odes, a Man may be oblig'd
to write thofe you know.

Luck. }
Wit. } Ha, ha, ha. That's true indeed.

B   *Luck.*

Luck. But about my Tragedy, Mr. *Marplay?*

Mar. jun. I believe my Father is at the Playhouse: If you please we will read it now; but I must call on a young Lady first———Hey! Who's there? Is my Footman there? Order my Chair to the Door——Your Servant, Gentlemen———*Caro vien.* [*Exit singing.*

Wit. This is the most finish'd Gentleman I ever saw, and hath not, I dare swear, his Equal.

Luck. If he has; here he comes.

SCENE VII.

Luckless, Witmore, Bookweight.

Luck. Mr. *Bookweight*, your very humble Servant.

Book. I was told, Sir, that you had particular Business with me.

Luck. Yes, Mr. *Bookweight*; I have something to put into your Hands. I have a Play for you, Mr. *Bookweight.*

Book. Is it accepted, Sir?

Luck. Not yet.

Book. Oh! Sir, when it is, it will be then Time enough to talk about it. A Play like a Bill is of no value till it is accepted: Nor indeed when it is, very often. Besides, Sir, our Playhouses are grown so plenty, and our Actors so scarce, that really Plays are become very bad Commodities. But pray, Sir, do you offer it to the Players or the Patentees?

Luck. Oh! to the Players, certainly.

Book. You are in the right of that: But a Play which will do on the Stage, will not always do for us; there are your Acting Plays, and your Reading Plays.

Wit. I do not understand that Distinction.

Book. Why, Sir, your Acting Play is intirely supported by the Merit of the Actor; in which Case it signifies very little whether there be any Sense in it or no. Now your Reading Play is of a different Stamp, and must have Wit and Meaning in't. These latter I call your Substantive, as being able to support themselves. The former

are

are your Adjective, as what require the Buffoonry, and Gestures of an Actor to be join'd with 'em to shew their Signification.

Wit. Very learnedly defined truly.

Luck. Well, but Mr. *Bookweight,* will you advance Fifty Guineas on my Play?

Book. Fifty Guineas! Yes, Sir. You shall have them with all my Heart, if you will give me Security for 'em. Fifty Guineas for a Play? Sir, I wou'd not give Fifty Shillings.

Luck. S'death, Sir! Do you beat me down at this rate?

Book. No, nor Fifty Farthings. Fifty Guineas! Indeed your Name is well worth that.

Luck. *Jack!* take this worthy Gentleman, and kick him down Stairs.

Book. Sir, I shall make you repent this.

Jack. Come, Sir, will you please to brush?

Book. Help! Murder! I'll have the Law of you, Sir.

Luck. Ha, ha, ha!

S C E N E VIII.

Luckless, Witmore, *Mrs.* Moneywood.

Money. What Noise is this? It is a very fine Thing truly, Mr. *Luckless,* that you will make these Uproars in my House.

Luck. If you dislike it, it is in your Power to drown a much greater. Do you but speak, Madam, and I am sure no one will be heard but yourself.

Money. Very well, indeed! fine Reflexions on my Character! Sir, Sir, all the Neighbours know that I have been as quiet a Woman as ever liv'd in the Parish I had no Noises in my House till you came. We were the Family of Love. But you have been a Nusance to the whole Neighbourhood. While you had Money my Doors were thundered at every Morning at Four and Five by Coachmen and Chairmen, and since you have had

none, my Houſe has been beſieg'd all Day by Creditors
and Bailiffs: Then there's the Raſcal your Man, but I
will pay the Dog, I will ſcour him.——Sir, I am glad
you are a Witneſs of his Abuſes of me.

Wit. I am indeed, Madam, a Witneſs how unjuſtly
he has abus'd you.   [Jack *whiſpers* Luckleſs.

Luck. Witmore, excuſe me a Moment.

SCENE IX.

Mrs. Moneywood, Witmore.

Money. Yes, Sir; and Sir, a Man that has never
ſhewn one the Colour of his Money.

Wit. Very hard, truly: How much may he be in your
Debt, pray? Becauſe he has order'd me to pay you.

Money. Ah! Sir, I wiſh he had.

Wit. I am ſerious, I aſſure you.

Money. I am very glad to hear it, Sir. Here is the
Bill as we ſettled it this very Morning. I always thought
indeed Mr. *Luckleſs* had a great deal of Honeſty in his
Principles; any Man may be unfortunate: But I knew
when he had Money I ſhou'd have it; and what ſignifies
dunning a Man, when he hath it not? Now that is a Way
with ſome People which I cou'd never come into.

Wit. There, Madam, is your Money. You may give
Mr. *Luckleſs* the Receipt.

Money. Sir, I give you both a great many Thanks. I
am ſure it is almoſt as charitable as if you gave it me; for
I am to make up a Sum to-morrow Morning. Well, if
Mr. *Luckleſs* was but a little ſoberer, I ſhould like him
for a Lodger exceedingly; for I muſt ſay, I think him a
very pleaſant good-humour'd Man.

SCENE X.

Luckleſs, Witmore, Moneywood.

Luck. Thoſe are Words I never heard out of that
Mouth before.

Money.

Money. Ha, ha, ha! you are pleas'd to be merry, ha, ha!

Luck. Why *Witmore,* thou haſt the Faculty oppoſite to that of a Witch; and can'ſt lay a Tempeſt. I ſhou'd as ſoon have imagin'd one Man cou'd have ſtopt a Cannon-Ball in its full Force, as her Tongue.

Money. Ha, ha, ha! he is the beſt Company in the World, Sir, and ſo full of his Similitudes.

Wit. *Luckleſs,* good Morrow: I ſhall ſee you ſoon again.

Luck. Let it be ſoon, I beſeech you; for thou haſt brought a Calm into this Houſe that was ſcarce ever in it before.

S C E N E XI.

Luckleſs, *Mrs.* Moneywood, Jack.

Money. Well, Mr. *Luckleſs,* you are a comical Man, to give one ſuch a Character to a Stranger.

Luck. The Company is gone, Madam; and now, like true Man and Wife, we may fall to abuſing one another as faſt as we pleaſe.

Money. Abuſe me as you pleaſe, ſo you pay me, Sir.

Luck. 'Sdeath! Madam, I will pay you.

Money. Nay, Sir, I do not ask it before it is due. I don't queſtion your Payment at all: If you was to ſtay in my Houſe this Quarter of a Year, as I hope you will, I ſhou'd not ask you for a Farthing.

Luck. Toll, loll, loll.———But I ſhall have her begin with her Paſſion immediately; and I had rather be the Object of her Rage for a Year, than of her Love for half an Hour.

Money. But why did you chooſe to ſurpriſe me with my Money? why did you not tell me you wou'd pay me?

Luck. Why, have I not told you!

Money. Yes, you told me of a Play and Stuff: But you never told me you wou'd order a Gentleman to pay me. A ſweet pretty good-humour'd Gentleman he is, Heav'n bleſs him. Well, you have comical ways with

you!

you: but you have Honefty at the Bottom, and I'm fure the Gentleman himfelf will own I gave you that Chara&er.

Luck. Oh! I fmell you now——You fee, Madam, I am better than my Word to you; did he pay it you in Gold or Silver?

Money. All pure Gold.

Luck. I have a vaft deal of Silver, which he brought me, within; will you do me the favour of taking it in Silver? that will be of ufe to you in the Shop too.

Money. Any thing to oblige you, Sir!

Luck. *Jack,* bring out the great Bag, Number *One.* Pleafe to tell the Money, Madam, on that Table.

Money. It's eafily told: Heaven knows there's not fo much on't.

Jack. Sir, the Bag is fo heavy, I cannot bring it in.

Luck. Why then, come and help to thruft a heavier Bag out.

Money. What do you mean?

Luck. Only to pay you in my Bed-chamber.

Money. Villain, Dog, I'll fwear a Robbery, and have you hang'd: Rogues, Villains!

Luck. Be as noify as you pleafe.—— [*Shuts the Door.*
Jack, call a Coach, and d'ye hear, get up behind it and attend me.

ACT

ACT II. SCENE I.

The Playhouse.

Luckless, Marplay *senior*, Marplay *junior*.

LUCKLESS. [*Reads.*]

"THEN hence my Sorrows, hence my ev'ry Fear;
"   No matter where, so we are bless'd together.
"With thee, the barren Rocks, where not one step
"Of human Race lies printed in the Snow,
"Look lovely as the smiling Infant Spring.

Mar. sen. Augh! Will you please to read that again, Sir?

Luck. " Then hence my Sorrow, hence my ev'ry Fear.

Mar. sen. " Then hence my Sorrow.—Horror is a much better Word.——And then in the second Line——" No " matter where, so we are bless'd together——Undoubtedly; it shou'd be No matter where, so somewhere we're together. Where is the Question, somewhere is the Answer——Read on, Sir.

Luck. With thee, &c.

Mar. sen. No, no, I cou'd alter those Lines to a much better Idea.

" With thee, the barren Blocks, where not a bit
" Of human Face is painted on the Bark,
" Look green as *Covent-Garden* in the Spring.

Luck. Green as *Covent-Garden*!

Mar. jun. Yes, yes; *Covent-Garden* Market, where they sell Greens.

Luck. Monstrous!

Mar. sen. Pray, Sir, read on.

B 4   *Luck.*

Luck. " *Leandra!* oh my Harmonio, I cou'd hear thee ftill;
    " The Nightingale to thee fings out of Tune,
    " While on thy faithful Breaft my Head reclines,
    " The downy Pillow's hard; while from thy Lips
    " I drink delicious Draughts of Nectar down,
    " *Falernian* Wines feem bitter to my Tafte.

Mar. jun. Here's Meat, Drink, Singing, and Lodg-
ing, Egad.

Luck. He anfwers.

Mar. jun. But Sir——

Luck. " Oh let me pull thee, prefs thee to my Heart,
    " Thou rifing Spring of everlafting Sweets;
    " Take notice, Fortune, I forgive thee all,
    " Thou'ft made *Leandra* mine; thou Flood of Joy
    " Mix with my Soul, and rufh thro' ev'ry Vein.

Mar. fen. Thofe two laft Lines again, if you pleafe.

Luck. " Thou'ft made, *&c.*

Mar. jun. " ——Thou Flood of Joy
    " Mix with my Soul, and rufh thro' ev'ry Vein.
Thofe are two excellent Lines indeed : I never writ better
myfelf: But, Sar——

Luck. " *Leandra's* mine, go bid the Tongue of Fate
.. " Pronounce another Word of Blifs like that;
    " Search thro' the eaftern Mines and golden Shores,
    " Where lavifh Nature pours forth all her Stores;
    " For to my Lot cou'd all her Treafures fall,
    " I wou'd not change *Leandra* for 'em all.
There ends Act the firft, and fuch an Act, as I believe
never was on this Stage yet.

Mar. jun. Nor never will, I hope.

Mar. fen. Pray, Sir, let me look at one thing.
    " *Falernian* Wines feem bitter to my Tafte.
Pray, Sir, what fort of Wines may your *Falernian* be ?
for I never heard of 'em before; and I am fure, as I
keep the beft Company, if there had been fuch Sorts of
Wines, I fhould have tafted 'em. *Tokay* I have drank,
and *Lacrimæ* I have drank, but what your *Falernian* is,
the Devil take me if I can tell.

Mar.

Mar. jun. I fancy, Father, thefe Wines grow at the Top of *Parnaffus.*

Luck. Do they fo, Mr. *Pert?* Why then I fancy you have never tafted them.

Mar. fen. Suppofe you fhou'd fay; The Wines of *Cape* are bitter to my Tafte.

Luck. Sir, I cannot alter it.

Mar. fen. Nor we cannot act it. It won't do, Sir, and fo you need give yourfelf no farther Trouble about it.

Luck. What particular Fault do you find?

Mar. jun. Sar, there is nothing that touches me, nothing that is coercive to my Paffions.

Luck. Fare you well, Sir: May another Play be coercive to your Paffions.

S C E N E II.

Marplay *fenior*, Marplay *junior*.

Mar. fen. Ha, ha, ha!

Mar. jun. What do you think of the Play?

Mar. fen. It may be a very good one, for ought I know; but I am refolv'd, fince the Town will not receive any of mine, they fhall have none from any other. I'll keep them to their old Diet.

Mar. jun. But fuppofe they won't feed on't.

Mar. fen. Then it fhall be cramm'd down their Throats.

Mar. jun. I wifh, Father, you wou'd leave me that Art for a Legacy, fince I am afraid I am like to have no other from you.

Mar. fen. 'Tis Buff, Child, 'tis Buff——True *Corinthian* Brafs: And Heav'n be prais'd tho' I have giv'n thee no Gold, I have giv'n thee enough of that, which is the better Inheritance of the two. Gold thou might'ft have fpent, but this is a lafting Eftate that will ftick by thee all thy Life.

Mar. jun.

Mar. jun. What shall be done with that Farce which was damn'd last Night?

Mar. sen. Give it 'em again to morrow. I have told some Persons of Quality that it is a good thing, and I am resolv'd not to be in the wrong: Let us see which will be weary first, the Town of Damning or we of being Damn'd.

Mar. jun. Rat the Town, I say.

Mar. sen. That's a good Boy; and so say I: But prithee, what didst thou do with the Comedy which I gave thee t'other Day, that I thought a good one?

Mar. jun. Did as you order'd me, return'd it to the Author, and told him it wou'd not do.

Mar. sen. You did well. If thou writest thyself, and that I know thou art very well qualified to do, it is thy Interest to keep back all other Authors of any Merit, and be as forward to advance those of none.

Mar. jun. But I am a little afraid of Writing; for my Writings, you know, have far'd but ill hitherto.

Mar. sen. That is, because thou hast a little mistaken the Method of Writing. The Art of Writing, Boy, is the Art of stealing old Plays, by changing the Name of the Play, and new ones by changing the Name of the Author.

Mar. jun. If it was not for these cursed Hisses and Catcalls——

Mar. sen. Harmless Musick, Child, very harmless Musick, and what, when one is but well-season'd to it, has no Effect at all: For my part I have been us'd to 'em.

Mar. jun. Ay, and I have been us'd to 'em too, for that matter.

Mar. sen. And stood 'em bravely too. Idle young Actors are fond of Applause, but take my Word for it, a Clap is a mighty silly empty thing, and does no more good than a Hiss; and therefore if any Man loves Hissing, he may have his three Shillings worth at me, whenever he pleases.   [*Exeunt.*

SCENE

S C E N E III.

A Room in Bookweight's *House.*

Dafh, Blotpage, Quibble, *writing at feveral Tables.*

Dafh. Pox on't, I'm as dull as an Ox, tho' I have not a Bit of one within me. I have not din'd thefe two Days, and yet my Head is as heavy as any Alderman's or Lord's. I carry about me Symbols of all the Elements; my Head is as heavy as Water, my Pockets are light as Air, my Appetite is as hot as Fire, and my Coat is as dirty as Earth.

Blot. Lend me your *Byfshe*, Mr. *Dafh*, I want a Rhime for Wind.

Dafh. Why there's blind, and kind, and behind, and find, and Mind: It is of the eafieft Termination imaginable; I have had it four times in a Page.

Blot. None of thofe Words will do.

Dafh. Why then you may ufe any that end in Ord, or And or End. I am never fo exact, if the two laft Letters are alike, it will do very well. Read the Verfe.

Blot. " Inconftant as the Seas, or as the Wind,

Dafh. What wou'd you exprefs in the next Line?

Blot. Nay, that I don't know, for the Senfe is out already. I would fay fomething about Inconftancy.

Dafh. I can lend you a Verfe, and it will do very well too.

  Inconftancy will never have an End.
End rhimes very well with Wind.

Blot. It will do well enough for the middle of a Poem.

Dafh. Ay, ay, any thing will do well enough for the middle of a Poem. If you can but get twenty good Lines to place at the Beginning for a Tafte, it will fell very well.

Quib. So that according to you, Mr. *Dafh*, a Poet acts pretty much on the fame Principles with an Oifter-woman.

Dafh.

Daſh. Pox take your Simile, it has ſet my Chaps a watering: But come let us leave off Work for a while, and hear Mr. *Quibble*'s Song.

Quib. My Pipes are pure and clear, and my Stomach is as hollow as any Trumpet in *Europe*.

Daſh. Come, the Song.

S O N G.

A I R, Ye Commons and Peers.

How unhappy's the Fate
To live by one's Pate,
And be forc'd to write Hackney for Bread?,
An Author's a Joke,
To all manner of Folk,
Wherever he pops up his Head, his Head,
Wherever he pops up his Head.

Tho' he mount on that Hack,
Old Pegaſus' *Back,*
And of Helicon *drink till he burſt,*
Yet a Curſe of thoſe Streams,
Poetical Dreams,
They never can quench one's Thirſt, &c.

Ah! how ſhou'd he fly
On Fancy ſo high,
When his Limbs are in Durance and Hold?
Or how ſhould he charm,
With Genius ſo warm,
When his poor naked Body's a cold, &c.

S C E N E IV.

Bookweight, Daſh, Quibble, Blotpage.

Book. Fy upon it, Gentlemen! what, not at your Pens? Do you conſider, Mr. *Quibble*, that it is a Fortnight ſince your Letter to a Friend in the Country was publiſh'd? Is it not high time for an Anſwer to come out? At this

rate,

rate, before your Anfwer is printed your Letter will be forgot. I love to keep a Controverfy up warm. I have had Authors who have writ a Pamplet in the Morning, anfwer'd it in the Afternoon, and anfwer'd that again at Night.

Quib. Sir, I will be as expeditious as poffible: But it is harder to write on this fide the Queftion, becaufe it is the wrong Side.

Book. Not a jot. So far on the contrary that I have known fome Authors choofe it as the propereft to fhew their Genius. But let me fee what you have produc'd, with all Deference to what that very learned and moft ingenious Perfon, in his Letter to a Friend in the Country, hath advanced. Very well, Sir; for befides that it may fell more of the Letter, all controverfial Writers fhould begin with complimenting their Adverfaries, as Prize-fighters kifs before they engage. Let it be finifh'd with all fpeed. Well, Mr. *Dafh*, have you done that Murder yet?

Dafh. Yes, Sir, the Murder is done; I am only about a few moral Reflexions to place before it.

Book. Very well: Then let me have the Ghoft finifhed by this Day Se'nnight.

Dafh. What fort of a Ghoft wou'd you have this? Sir, the laft was a pale one.

Book. Then let this be a bloody one. Mr. *Quibble*, you may lay by that Life which you are about; for I hear the Perfon is recovered: And write me out Propofals for delivering five Sheets of Mr. *Bailey*'s *Englifh* Dictionary every Week, till the whole be finifhed. If you do not know the Form, you may copy the Propofals for printing *Bayle*'s Dictionary in the fame manner. The fame Words will do for both.

Enter Index.

So, Mr. *Index*, what News with you?

Index. I have brought my Bill, Sir.

Book. What's here? for fitting the Motto of *Rifum teneatis Amici* to a dozen Pamphlets at Sixpence per each,

Six

Six Shillings——For *Omnia vincit Amor, & nos cedamus Amori,* Sixpence.——For *Difficile est Satyram non scribere,* Sixpence——Hum! hum, hum! Sum total, for Thirty-six *Latin* Motto's, Eighteen Shillings; ditto *English,* One Shilling and Nine-pence; ditto *Greek,* Four, Four Shillings.   These *Greek* Motto's are excessively dear.

Ind. If you have them cheaper at either of the Universities, I will give you mine for nothing

Book. You shall have your Money immediately, and pray remember that I must have two *Latin* Seditious Motto's, and one *Greek* Moral Motto for Pamphlets by to morrow Morning.

Quib. I want two Latin Sentences, Sir, one for Page the Fourth, in the Praise of Loyalty, and another for Page the Tenth, in Praise of Liberty and Property.

Dash. The Ghost wou'd become a Motto very well, if you wou'd bestow one on him.

Book. Let me have them all.

Ind. Sir, I shall provide them.   Be pleas'd to look on that, Sir, and print me Five hundred Proposals, and as many Receipts.

Book. Proposals for printing by Subscription a new Translation of *Cicero*   *of the Nature of the Gods and his Tusculan Questions,* by *Jeremy Index,* Esq; I am sorry you have undertaken this, for it prevents a Design of mine.

Ind. Indeed, Sir, it does not, for you see all of the Book that I ever intend to publish.   It is only a handsom Way of asking one's Friends for a Guinea.

Book. Then you have not translated a Word of it perhaps.

Ind. Not a single Syllable.

Book. Well, you shall have your Proposals forthwith; but I desire you wou'd be a little more reasonable in your Bills for the future, or I shall deal with you no longer; for I have a certain Fellow of a College, who offers to furnish me with Second-hand Motto's out of the *Spectator* for Two-pence each.

Ind.

Ind. Sir, I only defire to'live by my Goods, and I hope-
you will be pleas'd to allow fome difference between, a
neat frefh Piece piping hot out of the Claficks, and old
thread-bare worn-out Stuff, that has paft thro' ev'ry Pe-
dant's Mouth, and been as common at the Univerfities as
their Whores.

SCENE V.

Bookweight, Dafh, Quibble, Blotpage, Scarecrow.

Scare. Sir, I have brought you a Libel againft the
Miniftry.

Book. Sir, I fhall not take any thing againft them;
for I have two in the Prefs already.   [*Afide.*

Scare. Then, Sir, I have an Apology in Defence of
them.

Book. That I fhall not meddle with neither; they don't
fell fo well.

Scare. I have a Tranflation of *Virgil's Æneid*, with,
Notes on it, if we can agree about the Price.

Book. Why, what Price wou'd you have?

Scare. You fhall read it firft, otherwife how will you
know the Value?

Book. No, no, Sir, I never deal that way: A Poem
is a Poem, and a Pamphlet a Pamphlet with me. Give
me a good handfom large Volume with a full promifing
Title-Page at the head of it, printed on a good Paper
and Letter, the whole well bound and gilt, and I'll warrant its felling —— You have the common Error of Authors, who think People buy Books to read—No, no,
Books are only bought to furnifh Libraries, as Pictures
and Glaffes, and Beds and Chairs are for other Rooms.
Look-ye, Sir, I don't like your Title-Page; however to
oblige a young Beginner, I don't care if I do print it at
my own Expence.

Scare. But pray, Sir, at whofe Expence fhall I eat?

Book. At whofe? Why at mine, Sir, at mine. I am
as great a Friend to Learning as the *Dutch* are to Trade:
No one can want Bread with me who will earn it; therefore,

fore, Sir, if you pleafe to take your Seat at my Table, here will be every thing neceffary provided for you : Good Milk-porridge, very often twice a Day, which is good wholfom Food, and proper for Students : A Tranflator too is what I want at prefent; my laft being in *Newgate* for Shop-lifting. The Rogue had a trick of tranflating out of the Shops as well as the Languages.

Scare. But I am afraid I am not qualified for a Tranflator, for I underftand no Language but my own.

Book. What, and tranflate *Virgil?*

Scare. Alas! I tranflated him out of *Dryden.*

Book. Lay by your Hat, Sir, lay by your Hat, and take your Seat immediately. Not qualified! Thou art as well vers'd in thy Trade as if thou hadft labour'd in my Garret thefe ten Years : Let me tell you, Ftiend, you will have more Occafion for Invention than Learning here. You will be oblig'd to tranflate Books out of all Languages, efpecially *French*, that were never printed in any Language whatfoever.

Scare. Your Trade abounds in Myfteries.

Book. The Study of Bookfelling is as difficult as the Law; and there are as many Tricks in the one as the other. Sometimes we give a Foreign Name to our own Labours, and fometimes we put our Names to the Labours of others. Then as the Lawyers have *John-a-Nokes* and *Tom-a-Stiles*, fo we have Meffieurs *Moore* near St. *Paul's*, and *Smith* near the *Royal-Exchange.*

S C E N E VI.

To them Lucklefs.

Luck. Mr. *Bookweight*, your Servant. Who can form to himfelf an Idea more amiable than of a Man at the Head of fo many Patriots working for the Benefit of their Country ?

Book. Truly, Sir, I believe it is an Idea more agreeable to you, than that of a Gentleman in the *Crown-Office*

Office paying thirty or forty Guineas for abuſing an honeſt Tradeſman.

Luck. Pſhaw! that was only jocoſely done, and a Man who lives by Wit, muſt not be angry at a Jeſt.

Book. Look ye, Sir. If you have a mind to com-promiſe the Matter, and have brought me any Money——

Luck. Haſt thou been in thy Trade ſo long, and talk of Money to a modern Author? You might as well have talk'd *Latin* or *Greek* to him. I have brought you Paper, Sir.

Book. That is not bringing me Money, I own. Have you brought me an Opera?

Luck. You may call it an Opera, if you will, but I call it a Puppet-ſhow.

Book. A Puppet-ſhow?

Luck. Ay, a Puppet-ſhow, and is to be play'd this Night in *Drury-Lane* Playhouſe.

Book. A Puppet-ſhow in a Playhouſe.

Luck. Ah, why, what have been all the Playhouſes a long while but Puppet-ſhows?

Book. Why, I dont know but it may ſucceed; at leaſt if we can make out a tolerable good Title-Page: So, if you will walk in, if I can make a Bargain with you I will: Gentlemen, you may go to Dinner.

SCENE VIII.

Enter Jack-Pudding, *Drummer, Mob.*

Jack-P. This is to give Notice to all Gentlemen, La-dies and others, That at the Theatre-Royal in *Drury-Lane,* this Evening will be perform'd the whole Puppet-ſhow call'd *The Pleaſures of the Town*; in which will be ſhewn the whole Court of Nonſenſe, with abundance of Singing, Dancing, and ſeveral other Entertainments:-----Alſo the Comical and diverting Humours of Some-body, and No-body: *Punch* and his Wife *Joan,* to be perform'd by Figures; ſome of them Six foot high. God ſave the King.　　　　　　　　　　　　　[*Drum beats.*

C　　　　　SCENE

SCENE IX.

Witmore *with a Paper, meeting* Luckless.

Wit. Oh! *Luckless,* I am overjoy'd to meet you: Here, take this Paper, and you will be difcouraged from Writing, I warrant you.

Luck. What is it?———Oh! one of my Play-Bills.

Wit. One of thy Play-Bills!

Luck. Even fo———I have taken the Advice you gave me this Morning.

Wit. Explain.

Luck. Why, I had fome time fince given this Performance of mine to be Rehearfed, and the Actors were all perfect in their Parts; but we happen'd to differ about fome Particulars, and I had a defign to have given it over; 'till having my Play refus'd by *Marplay,* I fent for the Managers of the other Houfe in a Paffion, join'd Iffue with them, and this very Evening it is to be acted.

Wit. Well, I wifh you Succefs.

Luck. Where are you going?

Wit. Any where but to hear you damn'd, which I muft, was I to go to your Puppet-Show.

Luck. Indulge me in this Trial; and I affure thee, if it be fuccefslefs, it fhall be the laft.

Wit. On that Condition I will: But fhou'd the Torrent run againft you, I fhall be a fafhionable Friend, and hifs with the reft.

Luck. No, a Man who cou'd do fo unfafhionable and fo generous a thing, as Mr. *Witmore* did this Morning—

Wit. Then I hope you will return it by never mentioning it to me more. I will now to the Pit.

Luck. And I behind the Scenes.

SCENE

S C E N E X.

Luckless, Harriot.

Luck. Dear *Harriot!*

Har. I was going to the Playhouse to look after you: I am frightned out of my Wits; I have left my Mother at home with the strangest sort of Man, who is inquiring after you: He has rais'd a Mob before the Door by the oddity of his Appearance; his Dress is like nothing I ever saw, and he talks of Kings, and *Bantam*, and the strangest Stuff.

Luck. What the Devil can he be?

Har. One of your old Acquaintance, I suppose, in Disguise: One of his Majesty's Officers with his Commission in his Pocket, I warrant him.

Luck. Well, but have you your Part perfect?

Har. I had, unless this Fellow hath frighten'd it out of my Head again: But I am afraid I shall play it wretchedly.

Luck. Why so?

Har. I shall never have Assurance enough to go thro' with it, especially if they shou'd hiss me.

Luck. O! your Mask will keep you in Countenance, and as for hissing, you need not fear it. The Audience are generally so favourable to young Beginners: But hist, here is your Mother, and she has seen us. Adieu, my Dear, make what Haste you can to the Playhouse. [*Exit.*

S C E N E XI.

Harriot, Moneywood.

Har. I wish I cou'd avoid her, for I suppose we shall have an Alarum.

Mon. So, so, very fine: Always together, always catter-wauling. How like a Hangdog he stole off; and it's well for him he did, for I shou'd have rung such a Peal in his Ears——There's a Friend of his at my

Houſe

Houfe wou'd be very glad of his Company, and I wifh
it was in my Power to bring 'em together.

Har. You wou'd not furely be fo barbarous.

Mon. Barbarous, ugh! You whining puling Fool!
Huffy, you have not a Drop of my Blood in you. What,
you are in love I fuppofe?

Har. If I was, Madam, it wou'd be no Crime.

Mon. Yes, Madam, but it wou'd, and a Folly too.
No Woman of Senfe was ever in Love with any thing
but a Man's Pocket. What, I fuppofe he has fill'd your
Head with a pack of romantick Stuff of Streams and
Dreams, and Charms and Arms. I know this is the
Stuff they all run on with, and fo run into our Debts, and
run away with our Daughters.———Come, confefs, are
not you two to live in a Wildernefs together on Love?
Ah! thou Fool! thou wilt find he will pay thee in Love,
juft as he has paid me in Money. If thou wert refolv'd
to go a begging, why did you not follow the Camp?
There indeed, you might have carried a Knapfack; but
here you will have no Knapfack to carry. There indeed
you might have had the chance of burying half a Score
Husbands in a Campaign; whereas a Poet is a long-lived
Animal: you have but one chance of burying him, and
that is ftarving him.

Har. Well, Madam, and I wou'd fooner ftarve with
the Man I love, than ride in a Coach and Six with him I
hate: And as for his Paffion, you will not make me
fufpect that, for he hath given me fuch Proofs on't.

Mon. Proofs! I fhall die. Has he given you Proofs
of Love!

Har. All that any modeft Woman can require.

Mon. If he has given you all a modeft Woman can
require, I am afraid he has given you more than a modeft
Woman fhou'd take: Becaufe he has been fo good a
Lodger, I fuppofe I fhall have fome more of the Family
to keep. It is probable I fhall live to fee half a dozen
Grandfons of mine in *Grub-ftreet.*

SCENE

S C E N E XII.

Moneywood, Harriot, Jack.

Jack. Oh Madam! the Man whom you took for a Bailiff is certainly fome great Man; he has a vaft many Jewels and other fine things about him; he offer'd me twenty Guineas to fhew him my Mafter, and has given away fo much Money among the Chairmen, that fome Folks believe he intends to ftand Member of Parliament for *Weftminſter*.

Mon. Nay, then I am fure he is worth inquiring into. So, d'ye hear, Sirrah, make as much hafte as you can before me, and defire him to part with no more Money till I come.

Har. So, now my Mother is in purfuit of Money, I may fecurely go in purfuit of my Lover, and I am miftaken, good Mamma, if e'en you wou'd not think that the better Purfuit of the two.

In genĕrous Love tranfporting Raptures lie,
Which Age, with all its Treafures, cannot buy.

A C T III. S C E N E I.

The Playhoufe.

Enter Luckleſs *as* Maſter *of the Show, and* Manager.

Luck. IT'S very furprifing, that after I have been at all this Expence and Trouble in fetting my Things up in your Houfe, you fhould defire me to Recant ; and now too, when the Spectators are all affembled, and will either have the Show or their Money.

Man. Nay, Sir, I am very ready to perform my Covenant with you ; but I am told that fome of the Players do not like their Parts, and threaten to leave the Houfe : Some to the *Hay-Market,* fome to *Goodman's-Fields,* and others to fet up two or three more new Playhoufes in feveral Parts of the Town.

Luck. I have quieted all that, and believe there is not one engag'd in the Performance, but who is now very well fatisfied.

Man. Well, Sir, then fo am I : But pray what is the Defign or Plot ? for I cou'd make neither head nor tail on't.

Luck. Why, Sir, the chief Bufinefs is the Election of an Arch-poet, or as others call him a Poet Laureat, to the Goddefs of Nonfenfe. I have introduc'd indeed feveral other Characters, not intirely neceffary to the main Defign ; for I was affur'd by a very eminent Critick, that in the way of Writing great Latitude might be allow'd, and that a Writer of Puppet-fhows might take as much more Liberty than a Writer of Operas, as an Opera-Writer might be allow'd beyond a Writer of Plays.

As

As for the Scene it lies on the other Side the River *Styx*, and all the People in my Play are dead.

Man. I wish they may not be damn'd too with all my Heart.

Luck. Sir, I depend much on the Good-nature of the Audience, but they are impatient, I hear them knock with their Canes. Let us begin immediately : I think we will have an Overture play'd on this Occasion. Mr. *Seedo*, have you not provided a new Overture on this Occasion ?

Seedo. I have compos'd one

Luck. Then pray let us have it. Come, Sir, be pleas'd to sit down by me.

Gentlemen, the first thing I present you with is *Punchinello*.

[*The Curtain draws, and discovers* Punch *in a great Chair.*

Punch *sings.*

A I R I. Whilst the Town's brimfull of Folly.

Whilst the Town's brimful of Farces,
Flocking whilst we see her Asses
  Thick as Grapes upon a Bunch,
Criticks, whilst you smile on Madness,
And more stupid, solemn Sadness ;
  Sure you will not frown on Punch.

Luck. The next is *Punch*'s Wife *Joan.*

Enter Joan.

Joan. What can ail my Husband ? he is continually humming Tunes, tho' his Voice be only fit to warble at *Hog's Norton*, where the Pigs would accompany it with Organs. I was in hopes Death would have stopp'd his Mouth at last. But he keeps his old harmonious Humour even in the Shades.

Punch. Be not angry, dear *Joan* ; *Orpheus* obtain'd his Wife from the Shades, by charming *Pluto* with his Musick.

C 4   *Joan.*

Joan. Sirrah, Sirrah, should *Pluto* hear you Sing, you cou'd expect no lefs Punishment than *Tantalus* has: —— Nay, the Waters would be brought above your Mouth, to stop it.

Punch. Truly, Madam, I don't wish the fame Succefs *Orpheus* met with ; could I gain my own Liberty, the Devil might have you with all my Heart.

A I R II.

Joan, Joan, Joan, *has a Thund'ring Tongue:*
And Joan, Joan, Joan, *is a bold one.*
　　How happy is he,
　　Who from Wedlock is free:
For who'd have a Wife to fcold one ?

Joan. Punch, Punch, Punch, *pr'ythee think of your Hunch,*
　　Pr'ythee look on your great ftrutting Belly :
　　　Sirrah, if you dare
　　　War with me declare,
　　I will beat your fat Guts to a Jelly.

[They Dance.

A I R III.　Bobbing *Joan.*

Pun. Joan, *you are the Plague of my Life,*
　　A Rope wou'd be welcomer than fuch a Wife.
Joan. Punch, *your Merits had you but fhar'd*
　　Your Neck had been longer by half a Yard :
Pun.　　　*Ugly Witch,*
Joan.　　　*Son of a Bitch,*
Both. *Wou'd you were hang'd, or drown'd in a Ditch.*

[Dance again.

Pun. *Since we hate like People in Vogue,*
　　Let us call not Bitch and Rogue :
　　Gentler Titles let us ufe,
　　Hate each other, but not abufe.

　　　　　　　　　　　　　　Joan.

Joan.   *Pretty Dear!*
Pun.   *Ah! Ma Chere!*
Both. *Joy of my Life, and only Care.*

[Dance, and *Exeunt.*

Luck. Gentlemen, the next is *Charon* and a Poet; they are disputing about an Affair pretty common with Poets ——Going off without Paying.

Enter Charon, *and a* Poet.

Char. Never tell me, Sir, I expect my Fare. I wonder what Trade these Authors drive in the other World: I would with as good a Will see a Soldier aboard my Boat. A tatter'd Red-coat, and a tatter'd Black one have bilk'd me so often, that I am resolv'd never to take either of them up again——unless I am paid before-hand.

Poet. What a wretched thing it is to be Poor? My Body lay a Fortnight in the other World before it was Buried. And this Fellow has kept my Spirit a Month, sunning himself on the other side the River, because my Pockets were empty. Wilt thou be so kind as to shew me the Way to the Court of *Nonsense?*

Char. Ha, ha! the Court of *Nonsense!* why, pray, Sir, what have you to do there? these Rags look more like the Dress of one of *Apollo*'s People, than of *Nonsense*'s.

Poet. Why, Fellow, didst thou never carry Rags to *Nonsense?*

Char. Truly, Sir, I cannot say but I have, but it is a long time ago, I assure you. But if you are really bound thither, and are a Poet, as I presume from your outward Appearance, you shou'd have brought a Certificate from the Goddess's Agent, Mr. What-d'ye-call-him, the Gentleman that writes Odes——So finely! However, that I may not hear any more of your Verses on the River Side,

I'll

I'll e'en carry you over on her Account: She pays for all her insolvent Votaries. Look at that Account, Sir, She is the best Deity to me in the Shades.

Poet. *Spirits imported for the Goddess of* Nonsense.
 Five People of great Quality,
 Seven ordinary Courtiers,
 Nineteen Attorneys,
 Eleven Counsellors,
 One hundred Poets, Players, Doctors, and Apothecaries, Fellows of Colleges, and Members of the Royal Society.

Luck. Gentlemen, the next is one of *Charon's* Men with a Prisoner.

Enter Sailor, *and a* Sexton.

Cha. How now?
Sail. We have caught him at last. This is Mr. *Robgrave* the Sexton, who has plunder'd so many Spirits.
Cha. Are you come at last, Sir? What have you to say for yourself? Ha! Where are all the Jewels and other valuable things you have stolen? Where are they, Sirrah? Ha!
Sex. Alack, Sir, I am but a poor Rogue; the Parish-Officers and others have had them all; I had only a small Reward for stealing them.
Char. Then you shall have another Reward here, Sir. Carry him before Justice *Minos*; the Moment he gets on the other side the Water, let him be shackled and put aboard.
[*Exeunt* Sailor *and* Sexton.
Poet. Who knows whether this Rogue has not robb'd me too. I forgot to look in upon my Body before I came away.
Char. Had you any things of Value buried with you?

Poet.

Poet. Things of Ineſtimable Value; ſix Folio's of my own Works.

Luck. Moſt Poets of this Age will have their Works buried with them.

[*The next is the Ghoſt of a* Director.]

Enter Director.

Dir. Mr. *Charon,* I want a Boat to croſs the River.

Cha. You ſhall have a Place, Sir; I believe I have juſt room for you, unleſs you are a Lawyer, and I have ſtrict Orders to carry no more over yet: Hell is too full of them already.

Dir. Sir, I am a Director.

Cha. A Director! what's that?

Dir. A Director of a Company, Sir. I am ſurpris'd you ſhould not know what that is: I thought our Names had been famous enough on this Road.

Cha. Oh Sir, I ask your Honour's Pardon; will you be pleas'd to go aboard.

Dir. I muſt have a whole Boat by myſelf; for I have two Waggon-loads of Treaſure that will be here immediately.

Cha. It is as much as my Place is worth to take any thing of that Nature aboard.

Dir. Pſhaw, pſhaw, you ſhall go ſnacks with me, and I warrant we cheat the Devil. I have been already too hard for him in the other World——Do you underſtand what Security on Bottomry is? I'll make your Fortune.

Cha. Here, take the Gentleman, let him be well fetter'd, and carried aboard, away with him.

Sail. Sir, here are a Waggon-load of Ghoſts arriv'd from *England* that were knock'd on the Head at a late Election.

Cha. Fit out another Boat immediately: But be ſure to ſearch their Pockets, that they carry nothing over with them. I found a Bank-bill of fifty Pound t'other

Day

Day in the Pocket of a Cobler's Ghoſt, who came hither on the ſame Account.

2 Sail. Sir, a great Number of Paſſengers arriv'd from *London*, all bound to the Court of *Nonſenſe.*

Char. Some Plague, I ſuppoſe, or a freſh Cargo of Phyſicians come to Town from the Univerſities

Luck. Now, Gentlemen, I ſhall produce ſuch a ſet of Figures as I defy all *Europe*, except our own Playhouſes, to equal.—Come, put away ; pray mind theſe Figures.

Enter Don Tragedio, *Sir* Farcical Comick, *Dr.* Orator, Signior Opera, Monſieur Pantomime, *and Mrs.* Novel.

Poet. Ha! *Don Tragedio,* your moſt obedient Servant. Sir *Farcical!* Dr. *Orator !* I am heartily glad to ſee you, Dear *Signior Opera! Monſieur Pantomime!* Ha! *Mynheer Van-treble!* Mrs. *Novel* in the Shades too ! what lucky Diſtemper cou'd have ſent ſo much good Company hither?

Trag. A Tragedy occaſion'd me to die ;
That periſhing the firſt Day, ſo did I.

Farc. A Paſtoral ſent me out of the World. My Life went out in a Hiſs ; Stap my Vitals.

Ora. A Muggletonian Dog ſtabb'd me.

A I R IV. *Silvia,* my Deareſt.

Oper. Claps univerſal,
Applauſes reſounding ;
Hiſſes confounding
Attending my Song :
My Senſes drowned,
And I fell down dead ;
Whilſt I was Singing, Ding, dang, dong.

Poet. Well, Monſieur *Pantomime,* how came you by your Fate ?

Pantom.

Pantom. [*Makes Signs to his Neck.*]

Poet. Broke his Neck : Alas poor Gentleman !———
And you, Mynheer *Van-treble*, what sent you hither?

Poet. And you Madam *Novel* ?

A I R V. 'Twas when the Seas were roaring.

Nov.   *Oh! Pity all a Maiden,*
        Condemn'd hard Fates to prove;
    I rather would have laid-in,
        Than thus have died for Love !
    'Twas hard t'encounter Death-a,
        Before the Bridal Bed ;
    Ah! would I had kept my Breath-a,
        And lost my Maiden-head.

Poet. Poor Lady !

Cha. Come, my Masters, it is a rare fresh Gale ; if you please I'll shew you aboard.

Luck. Observe, Gentlemen, how these Figures walk off. The next, Gentlemen, is a Blackamore Lady, who comes to present you with a Saraband and Castanets.
                        [*A Dance.*
Now, Gentlemen and Ladies, I shall produce a Book-seller who is the prime Minister of *Nonsense*, and the Poet.

Enter Bookseller, *and* Poet.

Poet. 'Tis strange, 'tis wondrous strange!

Book. And yet 'tis true. Did you observe her Eyes?

Poet. Her Ears rather, for there she took the Infection. She saw the *Signior*'s Visage in his Voice.

Book. Did you not mark, how she melted when he Sung ?

Poet. I saw her like another *Dido.* I saw her Heart rise up to her Eyes, and drop down again to her Ears.

                                Book.

Book. That a Woman of so much Sense as the Goddess of *Nonsense*, should be taken thus at first Sight! I have serv'd her faithfully these thirty Years as a Bookseller in the upper World, and never knew her guilty of one Folly before.

Poet. Nay certainly, Mr. *Curry*, you know as much of her, as any Man.

Book. I think I ought, I am sure I have made as large Oblations to her, as all *Warwick-Lane* and *Pater-Noster-Row*.

Poet. But is she, this Night, to be married to *Signior Opera?*

Book. This is to be the Bridal Night. Well, this will be the strangest Thing that has hapned in the Shades, since the Rape of *Proserpine.*—But now I think on't, what News bring you from the other World?

Poet. Why, Affairs go much in the same Road there as when you were alive, Authors starve, and Booksellers grow fat, *Grub-street* harbours as many Pirates as ever *Algiers* did. They have more Theatres than are at *Paris*, and just as much Wit as there is at *Amsterdam*; they have ransack'd all *Italy* for Singers, and all *France* for Dancers.

Book. And all Hell for Conjurers.

Poet. My Lord-Mayor has shorten'd the Time of *Bartholomew*-Fair in *Smithfield*, and so they are resolved to keep it all the Year round at the other End of the Town.

Book. I find Matters go swimmingly; but I fancy I am wanted; if you please, Sir, I will shew you the way.

Poet. Sir, I follow you. [*Exeunt.*

Enter Punch.

Punch. You, Fidler.

Luck. Well, *Punch*, what's the Matter now?

Punch. What do you think my Wife *Joan* is about?

Luck.

Luck. Faith, I can't tell.

Punch. Odsbobs; she is got with three Women of Quality at Quadrille.

Luck. Quadrille! ha, ha!

Punch. I have taken a Resolution to run away from her, and set up a Trade.

Luck. A Trade? why, you have no Stock.

Punch. Oh, but I intend to break, cheat my Creditors, and so get one.

Luck. That Bite is too stale, Master *Punch.*

Punch. Is it? Then I'll e'en turn Lawyer. There is no Stock requir'd there, but a Stock of Impudence.

Luck. Yes, there is a Stock of Law, without which you will starve at the Bar.

Punch. Ay, but I'll get upon the Bench, then I shall soon have Law enough; for then I can make any thing I say to be Law.

Luck. Hush, you scurrilous Rascal.

Punch. Odsbobs, I have hit it now.

Luck. What now?

Punch. I have it at last; the rarest Trade. *Punch,* thou art made for ever.

Luck. What Conceit has the Fool got in his Head now?

Punch. I'll e'en turn Parliament-Man.

Luck. Ha, ha, ha! Why, Sirrah, thou hast neither Interest nor Qualification.

Punch. How! not Interest? Yes, Sir, *Punch* is very well known to have a very considerable Interest in all the Corporations in *England*; and for Qualification, if I have no Estate of my own, I can borrow one.

Luck. This will never do, Master *Punch*—You must think of something you have a better Qualification for.

Punch. Ay, why then I'll turn great Man, that requires no Qualification whatsoever.

Luck. Get you gone, you impudent Rogue.

Gentlemen, the next Figures are *Some-body* and *No-body,* come to present you with a Song and a Dance.

Enter

Enter Some-body, *and* No-body.

A I R VII. Black Joke.

Some. *Of all the Men in* London *Town,*
        Or Knaves, or Fools, in Coat, or Gown,
         The Reprefentative am I:
No.   *Go thro' the World, and you will find,*
       In all the Claffes of Human-kind,
       Many a jolly No-body.

For him, a No-body, *fure we may call,*
Who during his Life does nothing at all,
   But Eat, and Snore,
   And Drink, and Rore,
From Whore to the Tavern, from Tavern to Whore,
With a lac'd Coat, and that is all.

Luck. Gentlemen, this is the End of the firft Interlude.

Luck. Now, Gentlemen, I fhall prefent you with the moft glorious Scene that has ever appear'd on the Stage : It is *The Court of Nonfenfe.* Play away, foft Mufick, and draw up the Curtain.

The Curtain drawn up to foft Mufick, difcovers the Goddefs of Nonfenfe *on a Throne; the Orator in a Tub;* Tragedio, *&c. attending.*

Nonf. Let all my Votaries prepare
    To celebrate this joyful Day.

                          Luck.

Luck. Gentlemen, obferve what a Lover of *Recitativo*, *Nonfenfe* is.

Nonf. Monfieur *Pantomime!* you are welcome.

Pant. [*Cuts a Caper.*]

Nonf. Alas, poor Gentleman! he is modeft: you may fpeak; no Words offend, that have no Wit in them.

Maft. Why, Madam *Nonfenfe*, don't you know that Monfieur *Pantomime* is dumb? and yet let me tell you, he has been of great Service to you; he is the only One of your Votaries that fets People afleep without Talking. But here's *Don Tragedio* will make Noife enough.

Trag. Yes, *Tragedio* is indeed my Name, }
Long fince recorded in the Rolls of Fame, }
At *Lincoln's-Inn*, and eke at *Drury-Lane*. }
Let everlafting Thunder found my Praife,
And forked Light'ning in my Scutcheon blaze;
To *Shakefpear*, *Johnfon*, *Dryden*, *Lee*, or *Rowe*.
I not a Line, no, not a Thought, do owe.
Me, for my Novelty, let all adore,
For, as I wrote, none ever wrote before.

Nonf. Thou art doubly welcome, welcome.

Trag. That Welcome, yes, that Welcome is my Due,
Two Tragedies I wrote, and wrote for you;
And, had not Hiffes, Hiffes me difmay'd,
By this, I'd writ Two-fcore, Two-fcore, by Jay'd.

Luck. By Jay'd! ay, that's another Excellence of the Don's; he does not only glean up all the Bad Words of other Authors, but makes new Bad Words of his own.

Farc. Nay, i'gad, I have made new Words, and fpoil'd old ones too, if you talk of that; I have made Foreigners break *Englifh*, and *Englifhmen* break *Latin*. I have as great a Confufion of Languages in my Play, as was at the Building of *Babel*.

Luck. And fo much the more extraordinary, becaufe the Author underftands no Language at all.

Farc. No Language at all!——Stap my Vitals.

Nonf. Dr. *Orator*, I have heard of you,

Orat.

Orat. Ay, and you might have heard me too, I bawl'd loud enough, I'm sure.

Maſt. She might have heard you: But if ſhe had underſtood your Advertiſements, I will believe *Nonſenſe* to have more Underſtanding than *Apollo.*

Orat. Have underſtood me, Sir! what has Underſtanding to do? My Hearers would be diverted, and they are ſo; which could not be if Underſtanding were neceſſary; becauſe very few of them have any.

Nonſ. You've all deſerv'd my hearty Thanks——but here my Treaſure I beſtow. [*To* Opera.

Oper. Your Highneſs knows what Reward I prize.

A I R VIII. Lillibolera.

Op. Let the fooliſh Philoſopher ſtrive in his Cell,
By Wiſdom, or Virtue, to merit true Praiſe;
The Soldier in Hardſhip and Danger ſtill dwell,
That Glory and Honour may crown his laſt Days;
The Patriot ſweat,
To be thought Great;
Or Beauty all Day at the Looking-glaſs toil;
That popular Voices
May ring their Applauſes,
While a Breath is the only Reward of their Coil.

But would you a wiſe Man to Action incite,
Be Riches propos'd the Reward of his Pain:
In Riches is center'd all Human Delight;
No Joy is on Earth, but what Gold can obtain.
If Women, Wine,
Or Grandeur fine,
Be moſt your Delight, all theſe Riches can;
Would you have Men to flatter?
To be Rich is the Matter;
When you cry he is Rich, you cry a Great Man.

Nonſ. [Repeating in an Ecſtacy.]

When you cry he is Rich, you cry a Great Man.

Bra-

Braviſſimo ! I long to be your Wife.

Luck. Gentlemen, obſerve and take notice how the Goddeſs of *Nonſenſe* is ſmitten by Muſick, and falls in love with the Ghoſt of *Signior Opera.*

Novel. If all my Romances ever pleas'd the Ear of my Goddeſs—if I ever found Favour in her Sight—oh, do not rob me thus!

Nonſ. What means my Daughter?

Novel. Alas, he is my Husband!

Curry. But tho' he were your Husband in the other World, Death ſolves that Tye, and he is at Liberty now to take another; and I never knew any one Inſtance of a Husband here, who would take the ſame Wife again.

A I R IX. Whilſt I gaz'd on *Cloe* trembling.

Novel. *May all Maids from me take Warning,*
  How a Lover's Arms they fly :
  Leſt the firſt kind Offer ſcorning,
  They, without a Second, die.

  How unhappy is my Paſſion!
  How tormenting is my Pain!
  If you thwart my Inclination,
  Let me die for Love again.

Curry. Again! What, did you die for Love of your Husband?

Novel. He knows he ought to have been ſo.——He ſwore he wou'd be ſo.——Yes, he knows I dy'd for Love, for I dy'd in Childbed.

Orat. Why, Madam, did you not tell me all the Road hither, that you was a Virgin?

A I R X. Highland Laddy.

Oper. *I was told, in my Life,*
   Death, for ever,
   Did diſſever,

       Men

Men from ev'ry mortal Strife,
And that greatest Plague, a Wife.

For had the Priests possest Men,
　　That to Tartarus
　　Wives came after us,
Their Devil would be a Jest then,
And our Devil a Wife.

Nonf. Avaunt, polluted Wretch! begone ;
Think not I'll take Pollution to my Arms,
No, no,————no, no,————no, no, no.

Oper. Well, since I can't have a Goddess, I'll e'en
prove a Man of Honour. ———— I was always in Love
with thee, my Angel ; but Ambition is a dreadful Thing.
However my Ghost shall pay the Debts of my Body.

Novel. Now I am happy, verily.

Oper. My long-lost Dear !

Novel. My new-found Bud !

A I R XL. Dusty Miller.

Oper.　　*Will my charming Creature*
　　　　　Once again receive me?
　　　　Tho' I prov'd a Traitor,
　　　　　Will she still believe me?
　　　　I will well repay thee,
　　　　　For past Faults of Roving,
　　　　Nor shall any Day be
　　　　　Without Proofs of Loving.

　　　　On that tender lily Breast
　　　　　Whilst I lie panting,
　　　　Both together blest,
　　　　　Both with Transports fainting.

Both.　　*Sure no Human Hearts*
　　　　　Were ever so delighted !
　　　　Death, which others parts,
　　　　　Hath our Souls united.

A I R

AIR XII. Over the Hills and far away.

Op.　　*Were I laid on* Scotland's *Coast,*
　　　　　And in my Arms embrac'd my Dear,
　　　　Let Scrubbado *do its most,*
　　　　　I wou'd know no Grief or Fear.

Nov.　　*Were we cast on* Ireland's *Soil,*
　　　　　There confin'd in Bogs to dwell,
　　　　For thee Potatoes I wou'd boil,
　　　　　No Irish *Spouse shou'd feast so well.*

Op.　　　*And tho' we scrubb'd it all the Day,*
Nov.　　*We'd kiss and hug the Night away;*
Op.　　　Scotch *and* Irish *both shou'd say,*
Both.　　*Oh, how blest! how blest are they!*

Orat. Since my Goddess is disengaged from one Lover, may the humblest, yet not the least diligent of her Servants, hope she wou'd smile on him?

Luck. Master *Orator,* you had best try to charm the Goddess with an Oration.

Orat. The History of a Fiddle and a Fiddlestick is going to be held forth; being particularly desir'd in a Letter from a certain Querist on that Point.

A Fiddle is a Statesman: why? Because it's hollow. A Fiddlestick is a Drunkard: why? Because it loves Ros'ning.

Luck. Gentlemen observe how he balances his Hands; his Left Hand is the Fiddle, and his Right Hand is the Fiddlestick.

Orat. A Fiddle is like a Beau's Nose, because the Bridge is often down; a Fiddlestick is like a Mountebank, because it plays upon a Crowd.——A Fiddle is like a Stock-jobber's Tongue, because it sounds different Notes; and a Fiddlestick is like a Stockjobber's Wig, because it has a great deal of Horsehair in it.

Luck,

Luck. And your Oration is like yourſelf; becauſe it has a great deal of Nonſenſe in it.

Nonſ. In vain you try to charm my Ears, unleſs by Muſick.

Orat. Have at you then.

Maſt. Gentlemen, obſerve how the Doctor ſings in his Tub. Here are no Wires; all alive, alive, ho!

Orat. Chimes of the Times, to the Tune of *Moll Pately.*

AIR XIII. *Moll Pately.*

All Men are Birds by Nature, Sir,
Tho' they have not Wings to fly;
On Earth a Soldier's a Creature, Sir,
Much reſembling a Kite in the Sky;
  The Phyſician is a Fowl, Sir,
  Whom moſt Men call an Owl, Sir,
    Who by his Hooting,
    Hooting, hooting,
    Hooting, hooting,
    Hooting, hooting,
Tells us that Death is nigh.

The Uſurer is a Swallow, Sir,
  That can ſwallow Gold by the Jorum;
A Woodcock is Squire Shallow, *Sir;*
  And a Gooſe is oft of the Quorum:
  The Gameſter is a Rook, Sir;
  The Lawyer, with his Coke, *Sir,*
    Is but a Raven,
    Croaking, croaking,
    Croaking, croaking,
    Croaking, croaking,
After the ready Rhinorum.

Young Virgins are ſcarce as Rails, Sir;
  Plenty as Batts the Night-walkers go;
Soft Italians *are Nightingales, Sir,*
  And a Cock-Sparrow mimicks a Beau:

Like

Like Birds Men are to be Caught, Sir;
Like Birds Men are to be Bought, Sir:
   Men of a Side,
   Like Birds of a Feather,
   Will flock together,
   Will flock together,
Both Sexes like Birds will———too.

Nonf. 'Tis all in vain.

Trag. Is *Nonsense* of me then forgetful grown,
And muft the Signior be preferr'd alone?
Is it for this, for this, ye Gods, that I
Have in one Scene made fome Folks laugh, fome cry?
For this does my low bluft'ring Language creep,
At once to wake you, and to make you fleep?

Far. And fo all my Puns, and Quibbles, and Conun-
drums are quite forgotten, ftap my Vitals!

Or. More Chimes of the Times, to the Tune of *Rogues,*
Rogues, Rogues.

    A I R XIV.   There was a jovial Beggar.

The Stone that all things turns at will
   To Gold, the Chymift craves;
But Gold, without the Chymift's Skill,
   Turns all Men into Knaves.
         For a Cheating they will go, &c.
The Merchant wou'd the Courtier cheat,
   When on his Goods he lays
Too high a Price———but faith he's bit,
   For a Courtier never pays.
         For a Cheating they will go, &c.
The Lawyer, with a Face demure,
   Hangs him who fteals your Pelf;
Becaufe the good Man can endure
   No Robber but himfelf.
         For a Cheating, &c.

          Betwixt

Betwixt the, Quack and Highwayman-
  What-Difference can there be ?
Tho' this with Piftol, that with Pen,
  Both kill you for a Fee.

                For a Cheating, &c.

The Husband cheats his loving Wife,
  And to a Miſtreſs goes,
While ſhe at home, to eaſe her Life,
  Carouſes with the Beaus.

              For a Cheating, &c.

That ſome Directors Cheats were,
  Some have made bold to doubt ;
Did not the Supercargo's Care
  Prevent their finding out.

              For a Cheating, &c.

The Tenant doth the Steward nick,
  (So low this Art we find,)
The Steward doth his Lordſhip trick,
  My Lord tricks all Mankind.

              For a Cheating, &c.

One Sect there are to whoſe fair Lot
  No cheating Arts do fall,
And thoſe are Parſons call'd, God wot ;
  And ſo I cheat you all.

              For a Cheating, &c.

Enter Charon.

Char. An't pleaſe your Majeſty; there is an odd ſort
of a Man on t'other ſide the Water ſays he's recom-
mended to you by ſome People of Quality.———Egad
I don't care to take him aboard, not I.——— He ſays his
Name is *Hurloborumbo* —— *rumbo*——— *Hurloborumbolo,*
I think he calls himſelf, he looks like one of *Apollo's*
People in my Opinion, he ſeems to be mad enough to be
a real Poet.

Nonſ. Take him aboard.

Char. I had forgot to tell your Ladyſhip, I hear rare
News, they ſay you are to be declared Goddeſs of Wit.

                              Curry.

Curry. That's no News, Mr. *Charon.*

Char. Well, I'll take *Hurloborumbo* aboard.

[*Exit* Charon.

Orat. I muſt win the Goddeſs before he arrives, or elſe I ſhall loſe her for ever.——A Rap at the Times.

AIR XV.   When I was a Dame of Honour.

> *Come all who've heard my Cuſhion beat,*
>   *Confeſs me as full of Dulneſs*
> *As any Egg is full of Meat,*
>   *Or full Moon is of Fulneſs :*
> *Let the Juſtice and his Clerk both own,*
>   *Than theirs my Dulneſs greater ;*
> *And tell how I've harangu'd the Town,*
>   *When I was a bold Orator.*
>
> *The Lawyer wrangling at the Bar,*
>   *While the Reverend Bench is dozing,*
> *The Scribler in a Pamphlet War,*
>   *Or Grubſtreet Bard compoſing :*
> *The trudging Quack in Scarlet Cloke,*
>   *Or Coffee-houſe Politick Prater;*
> *Can none come up to what I have ſpoke,*
>   *When I was a bold Orator.*
>
> *The well-bred Courtier telling Lies,*
>   *Or Levée Hunter believing ;*
> *The vain Coquette that rolls her Eyes,*
>   *More empty Fops deceiving ;*
> *The Parſon of diſſenting Gang,*
>   *Or flattering Dedicator,*
> *Could none of them like me Harangue,*
>   *When I was a bold Orator.*

Enter Punch.

Punch. You, you, you.

Luck. What's the matter, *Punch?*

Punch. Who is that ?

Luck. That's an Orator, Maſter *Punch.*

Punch. An Orator——What's that ?

Luck. Why an Orator is—egad I can't tell what ; he is a Man that no body dares difpute with.

Punch. Say you fo, I'll be with him prefently. Bring out my Tub there. I'll difpute with you, I'll warrant. I am a *Muggletonian.*

Orat. I am not.

Punch. Then you are not of my Opinion.

Orat. Sirrah, I know that you and your whole Tribe would be the Death of me ; but I am refolv'd to proceed to confute you as I have done hitherto, and as long as I have Breath you fhall hear me ; and I hope I have Breath enough to blow you all out of the World.

Punch. If Noife will.

Orat. Sir, I ——

Punch. Hear me, Sir.

Nonf. Hear him ; hear him ; hear him.

A I R XVI. Hey *Barnaby*, take it for Warning.

Punch.   *No Tricks fhall fave your Bacon,*
          Orator, Orator, *you are miftaken ;*
          Punch *will not be thus confuted,*
          Bring forth your Reafons or you are nonfuited,
                    Heigh ho.
          No Tricks fhall fave your Bacon.
          Orator, Orator, *you are miftaken.*
Orat.   *Inftead of Reafons advancing,*
          Let the Difpute be concluded by dancing.
                    Ti, to.   [*They dance.*

Nonf. 'Tis all in vain : A Virgin I will live ; and oh great Signior, pr'ythee take this Chaplet, and ftill wear it for my fake.

Luck. Gentlemen, obferve how Signior *Opera* is created Arch-poet to the Goddefs of *Nonfenfe.*

Trag. And does great *Nonfenfe* then at length determine
          To give the Chaplet to that Singing Vermin ?

Nonf. I do.

Trag.

Trag. Then *Opera* come on, and let us try,
Whether fhall wear the Chaplet, You or I.

AIR XVII. Be kind and love.

Nov. *Oh, fpare to take his precious Life away;*
So fweet a Voice muft fure your Paffion lay:
Oh hear his gentle Murmurs firft, and then,
If you can kill him, I will cry Amen.

Trag. Since but a Song you·ask, a Song I'll hear;
But tell him, that laft Song·is his laft Prayer.

AIR XVIII.

Op. *Barbarous cruel Man,*
I'll fing thus while I'm dying, I'm dying like a Swan,
A Swan,
A Swan,
With my Face all pale and wan.
More fierce art thou than Pirates,
Than Pirates,
Whom the Sirens Mufick charms,
Alarms,
Difarms;
More fierce than Men on the high Roads,
On the high --- Roads,
On the high --- Roads.
More fierce than Men on the high Roads,
When Polly Peachum *warms.*
The Devil
Was made civil,
By Orpheus's *tuneful Charms;*
And can - - - - - -
- - - - - - - - - - - -n,
He gentler prove than Man?

Trag. I cannot do it——   [*Sheaths his Sword.*
Methinks I feel my Flefh congeal'd to Bone,
And know not if I'm Flefh and Blood, or Stone.

Pant,

Pant. [*Runs several times round the Stage.*]

Nonf. Alas, what means Monſieur Pantomime?

Curry. By his pointing to his Head, I ſuppoſe he would have the Chaplet.

Nonf. Pretty Youth!

Nov. Oh, my Dear, how ſhall I expreſs the Trouble of my Soul?

Op. If there be Sympathy in Love, I'm ſure I felt it; for I was in a damnable Fright too.

Nov. Give me a Buſs then.

A I R XIX. Under the Greenwood Tree.

In vain a Thouſand Heroes and Kings
    Should court me to their Arms,
In vain ſhould give me a Thouſand fine Things,
    For thee I'd reſerve my Charms:
On that dear Breaſt, intranc'd in Joy,
    Oh, let me ever be.

Op.   *Oh, how I will kiſs thee,*
    How I'll embliſs thee,
    When thou art a-bed with me.

Nonf. [*repeats*] *Oh, how I will kiſs thee, &c.*

    Alas! what mighty Noiſe?

Luck. Gentlemen, the next is a Meſſenger.

Enter Meſſenger.

Meſſ. *Stay, Goddeſs, nor with haſte the Prize bequeath,*
    A mighty Spright now haſtens here beneath;
    Long in the World your noble Cauſe he fought;
    Your Laureat there, your Precepts ſtill he taught.
    To his great Son he leaves that Laurel now,
    And haſtens to receive one here below.

Nonf. *I can't revoke my Grant, but he*
    Shall Manager of our Players be.

Luck.

Luck. The next is *Count Ugly* from the Opera-house in the *Hay-market.*

Enter Count Ugly.

Nonf. Too late, O mighty Count, you came.

Count. *I ask not for myself, for I disdain*
O'er the poor ragged-Tribe of Bards to reign.
Me did my Stars to happier Fates prefer,
Sur-Intendant dez plaisirs d'Angleterre ;
If Masquerades you have, let those be mine,
But on the Signior let the Laurel shine.

Trag. What is thy Plea ? Has't written?

Count. No, nor read.
But if from Dulness any may succeed,
To that and Nonsense I good Title plead,
Nought else was ever in my Masquerade.

Nonf. *No more, by* Styx *I swear*
That Opera the Crown shall wear.

A I R.

Nov. *Away each meek Pretender flies,*
Opera thou hast gain'd the Prize.
Nonsense grateful still must own,
Thou best support'st her Throne.
For her Subscriptions thou didst gain
By thy soft alluring Strain,
When Shakespear's *Thought*
And Congreve's *brought*
Their Aids to Sense in vain.

Beauties who subdue Mankind,
Thy soft Chains alone can bind;
See within their lovely Eyes
The melting Wish arise :
While thy Sounds inchant the Ear,
Lovers think the Nymph sincere;
And Projectors,
And Directors,
Lose a while their Fear.

Enter

Enter Charon.

Luck. How now, *Charon?* you are not to enter yet.

Char. To enter, Sir! Alack-a-day! we are all undone:
Here are Sir *John Bindover* and a Conſtable coming in.

Enter Sir John, *and* Conſtable.

Conſt. Are you the Maſter of the Puppet-Show?

Luck. Yes, Sir.

Conſt. Then you muſt along with me, Sir; I have a
Warrant for you, Sir.

Luck. For what?

Sir John. For abuſing *Nonſenſe*, Sirrah.

Conſt. People of Quality are not to have their Diver-
ſions libell'd at this Rate.

Luck. Of what do you accuſe me, Gentlemen?

Sir John. Shall you abuſe *Nonſenſe*, when the whole
Town ſupports it?

Luck. Pox on't, had this Fellow ſtaid a few Moments
longer, till the Dance had been over, I had been eaſy.
Harkye, Mr. *Conſtable*; ſhall I only beg your Patience for
one Dance, and then I'll wait on you?

Sir John. Sirrah, don't try to corrupt the Magiſtrate
with your Bribes: Here ſhall be no Dancing.

Nov. What does this Fellow of a Conſtable mean by
interrupting our Play?

A I R XXI.   Fair *Dorinda.*

Oh Mr. Conſtable,
 Drunken Raſcal,
Would I had thee at the Roſe.
 May'ſt thou be beaten,
 Hang'd up and eaten,
 Eaten by the Carrion Crows.
The Filth that lies in Common Shores,
 May it ever lie in thy Noſe,
  May it ever
  Lie in thy Noſe,
Oh may it lie in thy Noſe.

            Luck.

Luck. Mollify yourſelf, Madam.

Sir John. That is really a pretty Creature, it were a Piece of Charity to take her to myſelf for a Handmaid.

                                      [*Aſide.*

Conſt. Very pretty, very pretty truly ;——— If Magiſtrates are to be abus'd at this Rate, the Devil may be a Conſtable for me: Harkee, Madam, do ye know who we are ?

Nov. A Rogue, Sir.

Conſt. Madam, I'm a Conſtable by Day, and a Juſtice of Peace by Night.

Nov. That is a Buzzard by Day, and an Owl by Night.

AIR XXII. New-market.

Conſt. *Why, Madam, do you give ſuch Words as theſe*
    To a Conſtable and a Juſtice of Peace ?
    I fancy you'll better know how to ſpeak,
    By that time you've been in Bridewell *a Week ;*
      Have beaten good Hemp, and been
        Whipt at a Poſt ;
      I hope you'll repent, when ſome Skin
        You have loſt.
    But if this makes you tremble, I'll not be ſevere ;
    Come down a good Guinea, and you ſhall be clear.

Nov. Oh, *Sir John,* you, I am ſure, are the Commander in this Enterpriſe. If you will prevent the reſt of our Show, let me beg you will permit the Dance.

AIR XXIII. Charming *Betty.*

  Sweeteſt Hony,
    Good Sir Johny,
Pr'ythee let us take a Dance,
    Leave your Canting,
    Zealous Ranting,
Come and ſhake a merry Haunch.

Motions

Motions firing,
 Sounds inspiring,
We are led to softer Joys;
 Where in Trances
 Each Soul dances,
Musick then seems only Noise.

Sir John. Verily, I am conquer'd. Pity prevaileth over Severity, and the Flesh hath subdued the Spirit. I feel a Motion in me, and whether it be of Grace or no I am not certain. Pretty Maid, I cannot be deaf any longer to your Prayers, I will abide the performing a Dance, and will myself, being thereto mov'd by an inward working, accompany you therein, taking for my Partner that Reverend Gentleman.

Mast. Then strike up.

Enter Witmore, Moneywood, Harriot, Bantomite.

Wit. Long live his Majesty of *Bantam!*

Money. Heaven preserve him!

Bant. Your gracious Father, Sir, greets you well.

Luck. What, in the Devil's Name, is the Meaning of this?

Bant. I find he is intirely ignorant of his Father.

Wit. Ay, Sir, it is very common in this Country for a Man not to know his Father.

Luck. What do you mean?

Bant. His Features are much alter'd.

Luck. Sir, I shall alter your Features, if you proceed.

Bant. Give me leave to explain myself. I was your Tutor in your earliest Days, sent by your Father, his present Majesty *Francis* IV. King of *Bantam*, to shew you the World. We arriv'd at *London*, when one Day among other Frolicks our Ship's Crew shooting the Bridge, the Boat over-set, and of all our Company, I and your Royal Self were only sav'd by swimming to *Billingsgate*; but tho' I sav'd my Life, I lost for some time my Senses, and you, as I then fear'd, for ever. When I recover'd, after a long fruitless Search for my Royal Master, I set Sail for *Bantam,*

tam, but was driven by the Winds on far diſtant Coaſts, and wander'd ſeveral Years, till at laſt I arriv'd once more at *Bantam*, ——Gueſs how I was receiv'd—— The King order'd me to be impriſon'd for Life: At laſt ſome lucky Chance brought thither ſa Merchant, who offer'd this Jewel as a Preſent to the King of *Bantam*.

Luck. Ha! it is the ſame which was tied upon my Arm, which by good Luck I preſerv'd from every other Acci-dent, till want of Money forc'd me to pawn it.

Bant. The Merchant being ſtrictly examin'd, ſaid he had it of a Pawn-broker, upon which I was immediately diſpatch'd to *England*, and the Merchant kept cloſe Pri-ſoner till my Return, then to be puniſh'd with Death, or rewarded with the Government of an Iſland.

Luck. Know then, that at that Time when you loſt your Senſes, I alſo loſt mine. I was taken up half-dead by a Waterman, and convey'd to his Wife, who ſold Oiſters, by whoſe Aſſiſtance I recover'd. But the Wa-ters of the *Thames*, like thoſe of *Lethe*, had cauſ'd an entire Oblivion of my former Fortune.—— But now it breaks in like Light upon me, and I begin to recollect it all. Is not your Name *Gonſalvo?*

Bant. It is.

Luck. Oh my *Gonſalvo!* ⎫
Bant. Oh, my deareſt Lord! ⎬   [*Embrace.*

Luck. But ſay by what lucky Accident you diſcover'd me.

Bant. I did intend to have advertis'd you in the *Evening-Poſt*, with a Reward; but being directed by the Merchant to the Pawn-broker, I was accidentally there enquiring after you, when your Boy brought your Nab. (Oh, ſad remembrance, that the Son of a King ſhould pawn a Hat!) The Woman told me, that was the Boy that pawn'd the Jewel, and of him I learnt where you lodg'd.

Luck. Prodigious Fortune!

[*A Wind-horn without.*

E

Enter

Enter Meſſenger.

Meſſ. An Expreſs is arriv'd from *Bantam* with· the News ·of his Majeſty's Death.

Bant. Then, Sir, you are King.　Long live *Henry* I. King of *Bantam.*

Omnes. Long live *Henry* I. King of *Bantam.*

Luck. Witmore, I now may repay your Generoſity.

Wit. Fortune has repaid me, I am ſure more than ſhe ow'd, by conferring this Bleſſing on you.

Luck. My Friend —— But here I am indebted to the golden Goddeſs, for having given me an Opportunity to aggrandiſe the Miſtreſs of my Soul, and ſet her on the Throne of *Bantam.*　Come, Madam, now you may lay aſide your ·Mask ; ſo once repeat. your Acclamations, Long live *Henry* and *Harriot,* King and Queen of *Bantam.*

Omnes. Huzza!

A I R　XXIV.　Gently touch the warbling Lyre.

Harr.　Let others fondly court a Throne,
All my Joy's in you alone ;
Let me find a Crown in you,
Let me find a Sceptre too,
Equal in the Court or Grove,
I am bleſt, do you but love.

Luck.　Were I not with you to live,
Bantam *would no Pleaſure give.*
Happier in ſome Foreſt I
Could upon that Boſom lie.
I would guard you from all Harms,
While you ſlept within my Arms.

Harr.　Would an Alexander *riſe,*
Him I'd view with ſcornful Eyes.

Luck.　Would Helen *with thy Charms compare,*
Her I'd think not half ſo fair :
Dereſt ſhalt thou ever be.

Harr.　Thou alone ſhalt reign in me.

Conſt.

Conft. I hope your Majefty will pardon a poor ignorant Conftable: I did not know your Worfhip, I affure you.

Luck. Pardon you —— Ay more —— You fhall be chief Conftable of *Bantam*, ——You *Sir John*, fhall be chief Juftice of Peace; you, Sir, my Orator; you my Poet-Laureat; you my Bookfeller; you *Don Tragedio*, Sir *Farcical*, *Signior Opera*, and Count *Ugly*, fhall entertain the City of *Bantam* with your Performances; Mrs. *Novel*, you fhall be a Romance-Writer; and to fhew my Generofity, *Monfieur Marplay*, you fhall fuperintend my Theatres —— All proper Servants for the King of *Bantam.*

Money. I always thought he had fomething more than ordinary in him.

Luck. This Gentlewoman is the Queen's Mother.

Money. For want of a better, Gentlemen.

AIR XXV. Oh ponder well.

Money. *Alack how alter'd is my Fate!*
  What Changes have I feen! -
  For I, who Lodgings let of late,
  Am now again a Queen.
Punch. *And I, who in this Puppet-Shew*
  Have played Punchenello,
  Will now let all the Audience know
  I am no common Fellow.

Punch. If his Majefty of *Bantam* will give me leave, I can make a Difcovery which will be to his Satisfaction. You have chofe for a Wife, *Henrietta*, Princefs of *Old Brentford.*

Omnes. How!

Punch. When the King of *Old Brentford* was expell'd by the King of the *New*, the Queen flew away with her little Daughter, then about two Years old, and was never heard of fince. But I fufficiently recollect the Phiz of my Mother, and thus I ask her Bleffing.

Money.

Money. Oh, my Son!

Harr. Oh, my Brother!

Punch. Oh, my Sister!

Money. I am sorry, in this Pickle, to remember who I am. But alas! too true is all you've said: Tho' I have been reduced to let Lodgings, I was the Queen of *Brentford,* and this, tho' a Player, is a King's Son.

Enter Joan.

Joan. Then I am a King's Daughter, for this Gentleman is my Husband.

Money. My Daughter!

Harr. ⎫

Luck. ⎭ My Sister!

Punch. My Wife!

Luck. Strike up Kettle-Drums and Trumpets —— *Punch,* I will restore you into your Kingdom at the Expence of my own. I will send an Express to *Bantam* for my Army.

Punch. Brother, I thank you ————— And now, if you please, we will celebrate these happy Discoveries with a Dance.

A D A N C E.

Luck.   Taught by my Fate, let never Bard despair,

       Tho' long he drudge, and feed on *Grub-street* Air:

       Since him (at last) 'tis possible to see

       As happy and as great a King as me.

EPILOGUE.

1 Poet,	Mr. *Jones.*
2 Poet,	Mr. *Dove.*
3 Poet,	Mr. *Marſhal.*
4 Poet,	Mr. *Wells* jun.
Player,	Miſs *Palms.*
Cat,	Mrs. *Martin.*

Four POETS ſitting at a Table.

1 Po. **B**Rethren we are aſſembled here, to write
An Epilogue, which muſt be ſpoke To-night.
2 Po. Let the firſt Lines be to the Pit addreſs'd.
3 Po. If Criticks too were mention'd, it were beſt ;
With fulſome Flattery, let them be cramm'd,
But if they damn the Play————
1 Po————————————Let them be damn'd.
2 Po. Suppoſing therefore, Brother, we ſhou'd lay
Some very great Encomiums on the Play?
3 Po. It cannot be amiſs————
1 Po. ————————————Now mount the Boxes,
Abuſe the Beaus, and compliment the Doxies.
4 Po. Abuſe the Beaus!————But how?
1 Po. ————————————Oh! never mind.
In 'ev'ry modern Epilogue, you'll find
Enough, which we may borrow of that kind.
3 Po. What will the Name of Imitation ſoften?
1 Po. Oh! Sir, you cannot ſay good things too often ;
And ſure thoſe Thoughts which in another ſhine,
Become not duller, by becoming mine.
3 Po. I'm ſatisfy'd.
1 Po. ————The Audience is already
Divided into Critick, Beau, and Lady ;
Nor Box, nor Pit, nor Gallery, can ſhew
One, who's not Lady, Critick, or a Beau.

E P I L O G U E.

3 Po. *It muſt be very difficult to pleaſe*
  Fancies ſo odd, ſo oppoſite as theſe.
1 Po. *The Task is not ſo difficult, as put ;*
  There's one thing pleaſes all.
2 Po. *——What is that ?*
1 Po. *————— Smut.*
  For as a Whore is lik'd, for being tawdry,
  So is an Epilogue for——— ———
3 Po. [*in a Paſſion*] *——— I order you,*
  On Pain of my Departure, not to chatter,
  One Word ſo very ſav'ry of the Creature ;
  For, by my Pen, might I Parnaſſus ſhare,
  I'd not, to gain it all, offend the Fair.
1 Po. *You are too nice——for ſay whate'er we can,*
  Their Modeſty is ſafe behind a Fan.
4 Po. *Well, let us now begin.*
3 Po. *——— ——— But we omit*
  An Epilogue's chief Decoration, Wit.
1 Po. *It hath been ſo ; but that ſtale Cuſtom's broken ;*
  Tho' dull to read, 'twill pleaſe you when 'tis ſpoken.

Enter the Author.

Auth. *Fy, Gentlemen, the Audience now hath ſtaid*
  This half Hour for the Epilogue———
All Po. *——— ——— ———'Tis not made.*
Auth. *How ! then I value not your Aid of that,*
  I'll have the Epilogue ſpoken by a Cat.
  Puſs, Puſs, Puſs, Puſs, Puſs, Puſs, Puſs.

Enter Cat.

1 Po. *——— ——— ——— I'm in a Rage*
  When Cats come on, Poets ſhou'd leave the Stage.
          [Exeunt *Poets.*

Cat. *Mew, Mew.*
Auth. *——— Poor Puſs, come hither pretty Rogue,*
  Who knows but you may come to be in Vogue ?
  Some Ladies like a Cat, and ſome a Dog.

Enter

EPILOGUE.

Enter a Player.

Play. *Cafs!, cafs! cafs! cafs! Fy, Mr.* Lucklefs, *what*
    Can you be doing with that filthy Cat?   [*Exit* Cat.
Auth. *Oh! curft Misfortune——what can I be doing?*
    This Devil's coming in has prov'd my Ruin.
    She's driv'n the Cat and Epilogue away.
Play. *Sure you are mad, and know not what you fay.*
Auth. *Mad you may call me, Madam; but you'll own,*
    I hope, I am not madder than the Town.
Play. *A Cat to fpeak an Epilogue——*
Auth. ——————————*fpeak!——no,*
    Only to act the Epilogue in Dumb-Show.
Play. *Dumb-Show!*
Auth. ——— *Why, pray, is that fo ftrange in Comedy?*
    And have you not feen Perfeus *and* Andromeda?
    Where you may find ftrange Incidents intended,
    And regular Intrigues begun and ended,
    Tho' not a Word doth from an Actor fall;
    As 'tis polite to fpeak in Murmurs fmall,
    Sure, 'tis politer not to fpeak at all.
Play. *But who is this?*

Enter Cat *as a* Woman.

Auth. ——— ——— *I know her not* ———
Cat. ——— ——— ——— *I that*
    Am now a Woman, *lately was a Cat.*
                      [*Turns to the* Audience.
    Gallants, you feem to think this Transformation
    As ftrange as was the Rabbit's Procreation;
    That 'tis as odd a Cat fhou'd take the Habit
    Of breeding us, as we fhou'd breed a Rabbit.
    I'll warrant eating one of them wou'd be
    As eafy to a Beau, as ———*kiffing me.*
    I wou'd not for the World *that Thing fhould catch us,*
    Cries fcar'd Sir Plume.——— *Fore-gad, my Lord,*
       fhe'd fcratch us.

                                    Yet

EPILOGUE.

Yet let not that deter you from your Sport,
You'll find my Nails are par'd exceeding short.
But—Ha!—what Murmurs thro' the Benches roam!
The Husbands cry————we've Cat enough at home.
This Transformation can be strange to no Man,
There's a great Likeness 'twixt a Cat and Woman.

Chang'd by her Lover's earnest Prayers, we're told,
A Cat was, to a beauteous Maid of old.
Cou'd modern Husbands thus the Gods prevail on;
Oh gemini! what Wife wou'd have no Tail on.
Puss wou'd be seen where Madam lately sat,
And ev'ry Lady Townley be a Cat.

Say, all of you, whose Honey-moon is over,
What wou'd you give such Changes to discover;
And waking in the Morn, instead of Bride,
To find poor Pussy purring by your Side.
Say, gentle Husbands, which of you wou'd curse,
And cry, my Wife is alter'd for the worse?

Shou'd to our Sex the Gods like Justice show,
And at our Pray'rs transform our Husbands too,
Many a Lord, who now his Fellows scorns,
Wou'd then exceed a Cat by nothing—but his Horns.
So Plenty then wou'd be those Foes to Rats,
Henley might prove that all Mankind are Cats.

FINIS.

SD - #0039 - 230124 - C0 - 229/152/4 - PB - 9781333037291 - Gloss Lamination